Footpath Touring
with Ken Ward

The Cotswolds

Jog on, jog on, the footpath way,
And merrily hent the stile-a,
A merry heart goes all the day,
Your sad one tires in a mile-a.

William Shakespeare
The Winter's Tale

Jarrold Colour Publications, Norwich

About Footpath-Touring

This Footpath-Touring guide is designed to lead you easily along a walk which will show you the best of the North Cotswolds.

The route: The tour has been divided into daily stages that are well within the capabilities of those quite new to walking. More experienced walkers will, of course, extend these stages as they wish.

Lunches: The route is so arranged that every day but one there is a place where lunch can be obtained. (A reminder is included at the start of this day that you will need to ask for a packed lunch.)

Accommodation: Green information panels included on the maps contain advice on overnight accommodation. Unless mentioned, all will provide an evening meal. All have become known to me during my time of walking and research for this guide. I offer them in good faith, without accepting responsibility for them.

Those places where I received a particularly warm welcome are surrounded by a box.

The accommodation is divided into three price categories: economy, medium and not-cheap. All provide reasonable value while some can be outstandingly good. I suggest you always check costs when making reservations, and remember to check that VAT is included.

Where possible the exact locations of accommodation are indicated, however telephone numbers are given should directions be required.

Out of season it should be sufficient to make telephone reservations the day before. This gives you great flexibility in your programme allowing you to take non-walking days to suit inclinations and weather. In high holiday seasons reservations should be made as early as possible. (For non-walking days see page 3.) We recommend that you make it quite clear if an evening meal is required, and, if possible, give some indication of time of arrival.

Please mention Footpath-Touring when booking as all accommodations have been asked to suggest an alternative should they be fully booked.

All accommodations have been selected for their appreciation of the needs of Footpath-Touring walkers particularly regarding warm rooms, good food, drying facilities, early starts and packed lunches.

Where the accommodation is a pub or a licensed establishment this is indicated.

Two letters after the name show the period that accommodation is available, for example, A/O=April to October, M/N=March to November. Those open all year are identified with a □; however, remember that during winter months they may be decorating, taking holidays, or repairing burst water-pipes!

Footwear: I consider it essential to wear walking boots when Footpath-Touring in the Cotswolds. A few of the bridleway sections are well churned-up by frequent horse traffic, and consequently very muddy in wet periods, especially in those places shaded by trees. Boots will give the necessary ankle support, and well-cleated soles will provide a good grip and cushion the soles of the feet. Seek the advice of your local reputable outdoors shop, and select comfortable, lightweight walking boots, and wear them as much as possible before you begin Footpath-Touring. These boots are your wheels and you carry no spare – so choose wisely.

Waterproofs: I suggest that you assume that during your tour there will be wet days. However, rain is no hardship if you are properly protected.

You will need a lightweight waterproof jacket with hood, pockets and front opening. Lightweight waterproof over-trousers that can easily be slipped over booted feet are also essential. You are strongly advised to equip yourself with lightweight gaiters that go from boot to knee, and I suggest that you wear these on all but the driest days. Even when there is no rain they will protect trouser-leg bottoms from getting wet and

About Footpath-Touring

heavy from long, dew-laden grass or bridleway mud. And when you arrive at that welcoming hostelry, a flick of the wrist and you can step with confidence into even the lounge of the splendid Lords of the Manor hotel!

Non-walking days: If poor weather or other reasons oblige you to take a non-walking day, the next overnight stop can always be reached by taxi; telephone numbers of conveniently placed operators are included on the maps. Always check the fare first, and mention Footpath-Touring to benefit from any advantageous rates.

Maps: The maps in the guide, together with the route directions opposite, allow you to follow the route easily. However, you may wish to equip yourself with the excellent Ordnance Survey 1:50 000 maps, which will enable you to identify distant features. Sheets 150, 151 and 163 cover the whole route.

Guardian Angels: On some of the maps you will see reference to Guardian Angels. Should a situation develop during a day when a telephone call may become essential, you may call on these kindly Angels for help. They are all volunteers, of course, and any telephone calls made should be paid for.

This Cotswold Tour

You can complete this Footpath-Touring route in a week of easy walking, so that your programme might look like this:

> Saturday morning travel to Stratford-upon-Avon, with afternoon to explore this fascinating town with its many Shakespearian associations and perhaps go to the famous theatre. Commence walk on Sunday, and walk every day to arrive at Cheltenham on the following Sunday, and travel home.

However, if you have extra days to spare you could extend the tour in several ways. On the second day, for instance, you could end your walk at the interesting lunch-time venue of Chipping Campden where there is much worth seeing. The next day could well be a similar morning-only walk to attractive and popular Broadway. Instead of travelling home on arrival at Cheltenham, a day could be profitably spent in this once-elegant spa resort, thus making a ten or eleven day tour.

Footpath-Touring – An Introduction

You are strongly advised to read the 32-page book, *Footpath-Touring – An Introduction.* This gives a great deal of useful advice based on many years' experience of Footpath-Touring throughout the British Isles. It shows how baggage can be kept to the sensible and comfortable weight of about 11 lb *5 kg* for men and 10 lb *4.5 kg* for women. Advice is given on choosing walking clothes which will ensure comfort and safety, together with suggestions for lightweight evening wear; kit check-lists are included for both men and women. Hints are given on selecting a pack which will carry the load comfortably and efficiently. Other sections deal with medical kits, foot-care, choice of footwear, wet-weather clothing, necessities and luxuries. A chapter gives a brief history of the footpath system in Britain, how it has evolved over the centuries and how it is now protected by law. Finally, advice is given on making the most efficient use of the Footpath-Touring guide books, and how to ensure a successful and rewarding tour. A most useful acquisition! Available from good book-sellers for the low price of £1; or from the Publishers for £1.15 including postage and packing:

Jarrold Colour Publications, Barrack Street, Norwich NR3 1TR *or*
Footpath Touring, The Manor, Moreton Pinkney, Daventry, NN11 6SJ

Getting to Stratford-upon-Avon

By rail: Frequent service every day except Sunday.
Enquiries: Telephone 0788 60116. (Overseas enquiries:
British Rail, P.O. Box 100 London NW1). Ask for details of
Circular Saver fares, cheaper than two single fares.

By road/rail: A special coach service from Coventry station to Stratford-
upon-Avon operates every day except during February and
March. For details of this time-saving service contact: Guide
Friday, Civic Hall, Stratford-upon-Avon, telephone: 0789
294466.

By coach: National Express operate services throughout the year.
Enquiries: Telephone 0203 553737. (Overseas enquiries:
Mid'and Red Service Ltd, Pool Meadow Bus Station, Coventry
CV1 5EZ)

By car: Cars may be parked for the duration of your Footpath-Tour at
Arden Garages, Arden Street, Stratford-upon-Avon, (see
map). For details and rates: Telephone 0789 67446 and ask
for Christopher Titchmarsh.

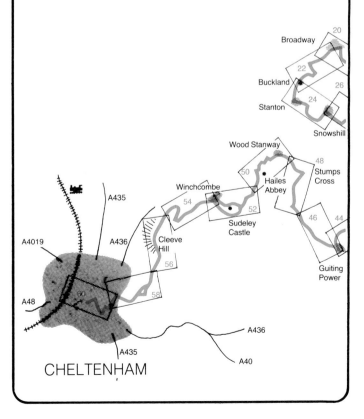

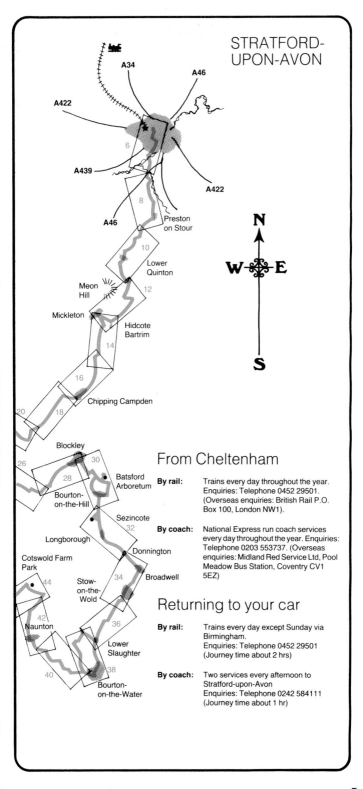

STRATFORD-UPON-AVON

A34
A46
A422
A439
A422
A46
Preston on Stour
Lower Quinton
Meon Hill
Mickleton
Hidcote Bartrim
Chipping Campden
Blockley
Batsford Arboretum
Bourton-on-the-Hill
Sezincote
Longborough
Donnington
Cotswold Farm Park
Broadwell
Stow-on-the-Wold
Naunton
Lower Slaughter
Bourton-on-the-Water

6 8 10 12 14 16 18 20 26 28 30 32 34 36 38 40 42 44

N W E S

From Cheltenham

By rail: Trains every day throughout the year. Enquiries: Telephone 0452 29501. (Overseas enquiries: British Rail P.O. Box 100, London NW1).

By coach: National Express run coach services every day throughout the year. Enquiries: Telephone 0203 553737. (Overseas enquiries: Midland Red Service Ltd, Pool Meadow Bus Station, Coventry CV1 5EZ)

Returning to your car

By rail: Trains every day except Sunday via Birmingham. Enquiries: Telephone 0452 29501 (Journey time about 2 hrs)

By coach: Two services every afternoon to Stratford-upon-Avon Enquiries: Telephone 0242 584111 (Journey time about 1 hr)

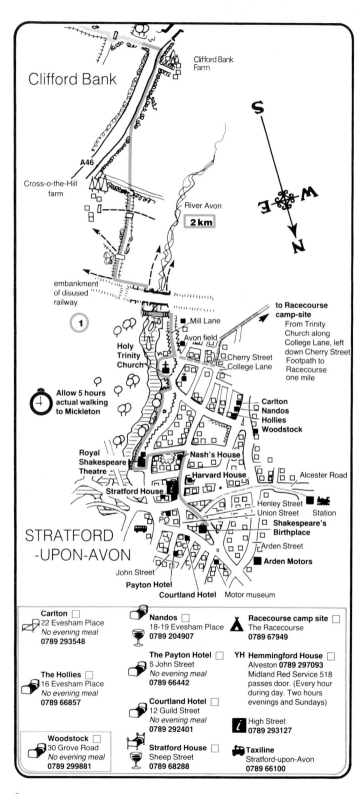

Clifford Bank

Clifford Bank Farm

A46

Cross-o-the-Hill farm

River Avon

2 km

S W E N

embankment of disused railway

(1)

Mill Lane

Avon field

Holy Trinity Church

Cherry Street
College Lane

to Racecourse camp-site
From Trinity Church along College Lane, left down Cherry Street Footpath to Racecourse one mile

Allow 5 hours actual walking to Mickleton

**Carlton
Nandos
Hollies
Woodstock**

Royal Shakespeare Theatre

Nash's House

Harvard House

Alcester Road

Stratford House

Henley Street
Union Street   Station

PO

Shakespeare's Birthplace

STRATFORD -UPON-AVON

Arden Street

Arden Motors

John Street

Payton Hotel

Courtland Hotel   Motor museum

Carlton ☐
22 Evesham Place
No evening meal
0789 293548

The Hollies ☐
16 Evesham Place
No evening meal
0789 66857

Woodstock ☐
30 Grove Road
No evening meal
0789 299881

Nandos ☐
18-19 Evesham Place
0789 204907

The Payton Hotel ☐
6 John Street
No evening meal
0789 66442

Courtland Hotel ☐
12 Guild Street
No evening meal
0789 292401

Stratford House ☐
Sheep Street
0789 68288

Racecourse camp site ☐
The Racecourse
0789 67949

YH Hemmingford House ☐
Alveston **0789 297093**
Midland Red Service 518
passes door. (Every hour
during day. Two hours
evenings and Sundays)

ℹ️ High Street
0789 293127

🚕 Taxiline
Stratford-upon-Avon
0789 66100

Lunch: The historic pub, College Arms, in Lower Quinton is roughly half-way (7 miles *11 km*) in this fairly long day, and is recommended.

Stratford to Clifford Bank Farm

Going The route through Stratford-upon-Avon begins at Shakespeare's birthplace, and ends at the church which houses his tomb. All the places mentioned are worthy of a visit, and this town walk could well be the subject of a special day, if time permits. Brief details with opening times are given on *page 62*. From the church by the River Avon, there follows an easy, though muddy, field walk with a short stretch of roadside pavement to Clifford Bank Farm.

By the Shakespeare Centre in Henley Street stands the cottage venerated for centuries as the birthplace of England's most famous poet and dramatist. *See page 62.*

From Birthplace, turn Left down Henley Street, and turn Right into High Street, by Information Centre in Judith Shakespeare's House. Along on Right is half-timbered Garrick Inn looking very much as it probably did four centuries ago. Next door is Harvard House. *See page 63.*

Continue ahead into Chapel Street, with Town Hall on Left-hand corner. At end of Chapel Street, on Left are Nash's House and New Place. *See page 62.*

From New Place turn Left into Chapel Lane. After a few paces, there is a pleasant diversion Left, through a gate into gardens on site of New Place's kitchen gardens and orchard; leave by gate further along. At end of Chapel Lane, cross road to Swan Theatre and Royal Shakespeare Theatre Museum and Gallery. *See page 63.* Turn Left to go around front of Theatre and turn Right on paved way between Theatre and river.

The River Terrace coffee shop is open every day during theatre season, except Sundays. 10.30a.m. – 11p.m.

Follow attractive riverside path, past Brass Rubbing Centre. At wall, turn Right to road, turn Left, and in few yards turn Left into churchyard. *See page 63.*

Follow riverside path round churchyard and leave opposite Avon Field, where turn Left down narrow, walled lane. Cross footbridge over Avon and turn Right along bank, below old railway bridge. Turn Left along path by old railway embankment, and in few yards turn Right along fenced and narrow, hedged field path, which rises to cross muddy track from Cross-o-the Hill farm. At kiss-gate in hedge, cross farm track and proceed half Left on path through crops to gap in hedge onto A46 Stratford to Mickleton road.

Turn Right onto pavement, and continue to Clifford Bank Farm. Here, with great care, cross busy road to Clifford farm track.

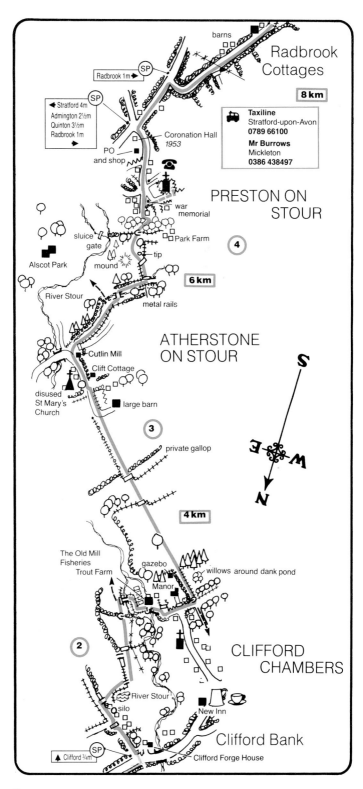

barns

Radbrook Cottages

8 km

Radbrook 1m ➤ SP

◄ Stratford 4m
Admington 2½m
Quinton 3½m
Radbrook 1m ➤

SP

Taxiline
Stratford-upon-Avon
0789 66100

Mr Burrows
Mickleton
0386 438497

Coronation Hall
1953

PO
and shop

PRESTON ON STOUR

war memorial

sluice gate

Park Farm

4

Alscot Park

mound

tip

6 km

River Stour

metal rails

ATHERSTONE ON STOUR

Cutlin Mill

Clift Cottage

S

disused
St Mary's
Church

large barn

3

private gallop

4 km

E W

N

The Old Mill
Fisheries
Trout Farm

gazebo

willows around dank pond

Manor

CLIFFORD CHAMBERS

2

River Stour

silo

New Inn

Clifford Bank

▲ Clifford ¾m SP

Clifford Forge House

8

Clifford Bank Farm to Radbrook Cottages

Going: A pleasant, level, well-walked field path through three small villages on the River Stour.

Continue up Clifford farm track. Just beyond farmyard and silos, turn Right through gate and down field with fence on Right. Over stile in field corner and turn Left along hedge to pass through muddy gateway. Down field just to Left of line of electricity poles and through kiss-gate in hedge. Cross small paddock to gate guarding bridge over the River Stour. Over bridge turn sharp Right to follow fenced path around tanks of Clifford Mill trout farm.

Ten tons of trout are reared annually in tanks through which flow one million gallons of water a day. It takes owner, Barrie Spratt, nine months to turn a one-ounce fingerling into a twelve-ounce trout. Very fresh rainbow trout and home-made trout paté on sale, *9.30a.m. – 4.30 p.m., Mon – Sat.*

Cross mill race in front of Mill and follow lane around to end of main street of Clifford Chambers. Cross this street with large gates of Clifford Manor on Left. Continue up avenue for few yards until wall on Left ends, and go Left through kiss-gate. Along fenced path to emerge between ruined gazebo on Left, and fir trees on Right. Continue straight ahead on field path, passing through two gates.

On fine days you are treated to free parachuting and wing-gliding displays over on your Right, from Long Marston airfield.

Join farm track near large barn at Atherstone on Stour. Follow farm track to pass on your Left large horse chestnut tree, disused church, and Atherstone Farm. Where track turns Left over bridge, turn Right on footpath past thatched and timber-framed cottage of Cutlin Mill.

The path between stream and fence is sometimes rather overgrown but always passable. At small stone culvert, stream switches to Right of path. At metal rail and footbridge on Right, turn Left through gate into field and continue with fence on Left. After few yards, through gate on Left, then same direction to locate kiss-gate in copse ahead.

The path meanders through copse, then leads into village of Preston on Stour by village green and war memorial.

A visit to the church of St Mary the Virgin is recommended. The Tower is fifteenth century and the rest dates from 1752–57. There are gilt royal arms of the Stuarts on the gallery, and fine memorials. Note the surprisingly lightly clad ladies in the Flemish glass of the east window. The unusual crucifix was created of driftwood taken from the beach in front of the Isle of Wight holiday home of General Sir Michael West, Knight Grand Cross, Order of the Bath.

Along village street, village shop/post office on Left. At cross-roads turn Right, (signposted Radbrook one mile). In few yards take Right turn, for a twenty-minute walk along quiet lane, with Radbrook Cottages on Left.

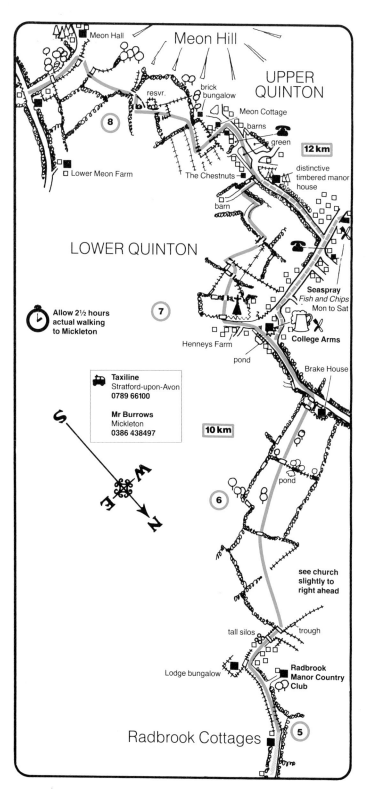

Meon Hall

Meon Hill

UPPER QUINTON

resvr.

brick bungalow

Meon Cottage

barns

green

12 km

⑧

distinctive timbered manor house

Lower Meon Farm

The Chestnuts

barn

LOWER QUINTON

Seaspray
Fish and Chips
Mon to Sat

Allow 2½ hours actual walking to Mickleton

⑦

College Arms

Henneys Farm

pond

Brake House

Taxiline
Stratford-upon-Avon
0789 66100

Mr Burrows
Mickleton
0386 438497

10 km

pond

⑥

see church slightly to right ahead

S

W

E

N

tall silos

trough

Lodge bungalow

Radbrook Manor Country Club

Radbrook Cottages

⑤

Radbrook Cottages to Meon Hill

Going: Easy field walking to Lower Quinton with its lunch-time pub, (and fish and chip shop), followed by a gentle climb to skirt Meon Hill (636 feet *194 m),* outlier of the Cotswolds.

Continue along lane, Radbrook Manor Country Club on Right. Just before bungalow on Left, turn Right into farmyard between barns and tall silos. Farmer often inconsiderately obstructs his mucky farm drive with gates to make cattle pens, but press ahead over gates and through puzzled cattle! Over final gate into cropped field, where turn half Left. Across field to pass through gap between hedge and fence. Continue same line over next cropped field and through gate in hedge. (See church slightly to Right ahead.) Cross next cropped field with two trees on Left, and through gate to Left of pond encircled with trees. Continue across next cropped field, with two trees on Right. (Stone debris suggests this was once paved route.) At Brake House, through two gates (pleasant contrast to farm), and turn Left on lane into Lower Quinton.

The welcoming College Arms inn (speciality gammon and eggs), was given by Henry VIII to Magdalen College, Oxford. The fine church of St Swithin's with its 127 foot *39 m* spire should be visited. Egbert, King of Wessex, caused a nunnery to be established here in the ninth century. Note the beautiful brass and tomb of Joan, Lady Clopton, and effigy of Sir William Clopton, who fought at Agincourt. There are the Royal Arms of Queen Elizabeth on the chancel arch, and splendid windows, with insects, birds and elves included at the suggestion of schoolchildren. *Good guide-book.*

Leave village through stile at rear of churchyard. Continue across field to stile and foot-bridge. Turn Left over stile and Right to cross field, in same direction, to Left of poles.

Until recently, the only remains of the ancient nunnery was a paved causeway over this once undrained meadow, which ran from the church door towards Upper Quinton. Unbelievably, a few years ago the farmer was allowed to plough away this historic relic!

At double stile, turn Left to follow hedge, and follow good track eventually onto road opposite fine timbered manor house, where turn Left to continue up Upper Quinton village green. At far end of green, onto road, and leave along passage to Left between Little Haven and Meon Cottage. Over stile into sheep paddock and over second stile to turn Right up to stile by brick bungalow. Over stile turn half Left and steeply up across field.

This corrugated field is a fine example of medieval 'ridge-and-furrow', which resulted from years of ploughing in strips. The strips were roughly 220 yards *200 m* long (a furrow long or furlong), said to be the distance that an ox team could pull a plough without pausing for breath. Meon Hill looms ahead.

At top Left-hand corner, into fenced pen and over corner stile into next field. Follow hedge on Right and over far corner stile. In few paces turn Left over stile and follow hedge on Left until it drops away on Left, and continue up middle of field. On crown of hill, firs and Meon Hall come into view. Drop down to cross two stiles and turn Left on farm drive.

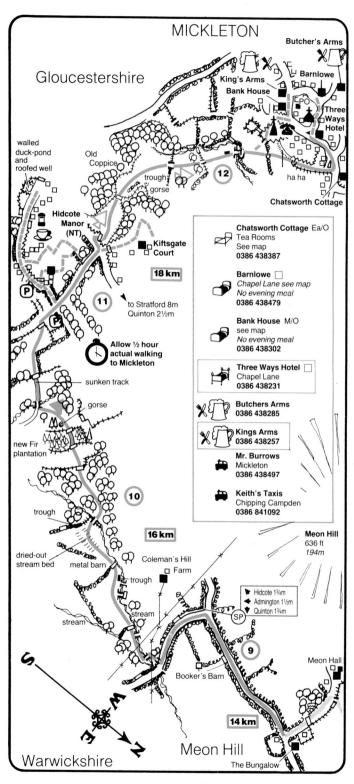

MICKLETON

Gloucestershire

Butcher's Arms

King's Arms
Bank House

Barnlowe

LPO

Three
Ways
Hotel

ha ha

Chatsworth Cottage

walled
duck-pond
and
roofed well

Old
Coppice

trough
gorse

12

Hidcote
Manor
(NT)

Kiftsgate
Court

18 km

P

11

to Stratford 8m
Quinton 2½m

P

Allow ½ hour
actual walking
to Mickleton

sunken track

gorse

new Fir
plantation

10

trough

16 km

dried-out
stream bed

metal barn

trough

Coleman's Hill
Farm

Meon Hill
636 ft
194m

stream

stream

SP

Hidcote 1¾m
Admington 1½m
Quinton 1¾m

9

Meon Hall

Booker's Barn

14 km

Warwickshire

Meon Hill

The Bungalow

Chatsworth Cottage Ea/O
Tea Rooms
See map
0386 438387

Barnlowe ☐
Chapel Lane see map
No evening meal
0386 438479

Bank House M/O
see map
No evening meal
0386 438302

Three Ways Hotel ☐
Chapel Lane
0386 438231

Butchers Arms
0386 438285

Kings Arms
0386 438257

Mr. Burrows
Mickleton
0386 438497

Keith's Taxis
Chipping Campden
0386 841092

Meon Hill to Mickleton

Going: A lane walk leads to footpath which gently climbs 643 feet *98 m* up Hidcote Combe to Hidcote Bartrim, and the famous National Trust gardens; then easily down into Mickleton village.

Continue along farm drive and turn Right at bungalow. Turn Left at junction. In about 400 yards *365 m,* just before bridge and trees, turn Right over fence, and after about 15 paces, Left to cross footbridge over stream – from Warwickshire into Gloucestershire.

Follow Right-hand stream through two field gates. From grassy trough of dried-out stream, bear Right up to corner of field and cross stile into copse. Follow path through copse and leave at gate. Cross field to join wide path that runs through small plantation of young firs. From plantation, past two fir trees and gorse on Left. Ascend valley. To Right of two trees, cross ditch by stone foot-bridge. Follow tractor tracks and sunken track into next field and emerge onto lane by Hidcote Manor car parks. Turn Right. Detour Left into Hidcote Bartrim if you plan to visit the gardens.

Beyond the entrance to the gardens is a populated duckpond and a walled well. The delightful and internationally famous gardens of Hidcote Manor are the result of over forty years work by the American, Major Lawrence Johnston, who presented them to the National Trust in 1948. The design consists of a series of separate gardens, both formal and informal, with names like 'White Garden', 'Fuchsia Garden', 'Stream Garden', 'Bathing Pool Garden', and all screened by hedges of yew, holly and hornbeam. Rare trees, shrubs and plants have been skilfully chosen to give a show of colour throughout the year. Although this has been a full day, do visit if possible; Mickleton is only half an hour down hill from here, and it makes a rewarding end to this first day. *From Easter – end Oct, open every day except Tues and Fri, from 11a.m. No admissions after 7p.m. National Trust shop. Tea room.*

Continue along road to T junction at Kiftsgate Court.

Kiftsgate Court gardens are dramatically arranged on a slope that runs down to Mickleton. There are trees, shrubs, flower beds and a superb display of old-fashioned roses. Refreshments are available. When the large Victorian house was built here in the 1880s the eighteenth-century Georgian portico of Mickleton Manor was transported from the village below by a specially constructed railway. *From Easter – end Sept, open Wed, Thur, and Sun, 2p.m.–6p.m.*

On Left of Kiftsgate drive is gated access to bridleway to Mickleton. Route drops down field to pass through very muddy gateway at gap in woods. No obvious track, but continue ahead to cross stile in fence, by water trough. Straight down field to cross fence by stile in centre of four trees. Cross field and through kiss-gate in hedge. Bear Right to kiss-gate in hedge just to Right of churchyard wall. *(For accommodation in village Left of church, take path through churchyard.)* Follow ha-ha which forms rear boundary to gardens. Through kiss-gate onto fenced path leading to main road, and turn Left into Mickleton. (Busy road so take care.)

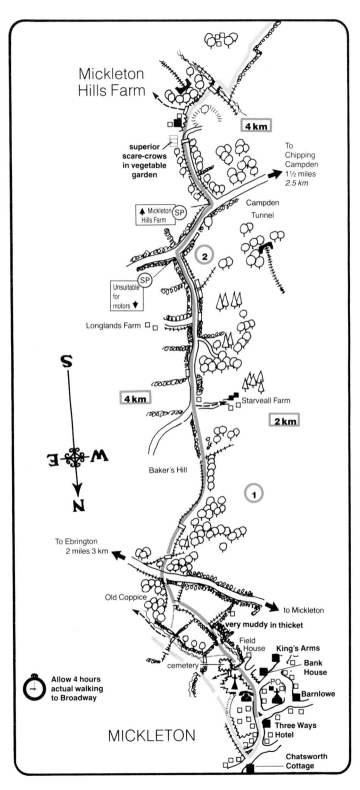

Mickleton
Hills Farm

superior
scare-crows
in vegetable
garden

4 km

To
Chipping
Campden
1½ miles
2.5 km

▲ Mickleton
Hills Farm SP

Campden
Tunnel

2

Unsuitable
for
motors ▼ SP

Longlands Farm ▢ ▢

S

4 km

Starveall Farm

2 km

W   E

Baker's Hill

N

1

To Ebrington
2 miles 3 km

Old Coppice

to Mickleton

very muddy in thicket

Field
House

King's Arms

Bank
House

cemetery

PO

Barnlowe

Allow 4 hours
actual walking
to Broadway

Three Ways
Hotel

MICKLETON

Chatsworth
Cottage

Lunch: The charming town of Chipping Campden (4 miles *7 km*) offers a wide choice of suitable establishments. *See page 16.*

Mickleton to Mickleton Hills Farm

Going: The field path from Mickleton to the road at Old Coppice can be extremely muddy. (A semi-official alternative is suggested during wet periods.) Once having gained the woods at Bakers Hill – an ascent of 250 feet *75 m* – there follows a very easy, level walk, with fine views to the west.

An attractive little Victorian fountain by Three Ways commemorates the man – and his daughter – who first brought water to the village.

Leave village by little lane leading to church.

This is another church which will enrich your tour. St Lawrence's 90 foot *28 m* spire dates from the fourteenth century. The porch with an upper room chapel (seventeenth century) was used by the £20-a-year schoolmaster to teach poor boys of the parish from 1665 to 1857. The stone crucifix in the window dates from the twelfth century. There are several coats of arms of the Graves family in the North Aisle chapel, including the motto *'Aquila non captat muscas'* – 'An eagle does not catch flies'. *Interesting guide-book.*

At walled cemetery opposite church, climb up to Right to pass through kiss-gate. Cross field diagonally to find small gate and footbridge hidden in corner. The path through thicket is usually very muddy, and in fact sometimes resembles a stream. *(See note below.)* Once clear of thicket, continue up length of field with hedge on Left. At muddy gap in fence, turn half Right across field, and over stile in corner to road.

Note: **To avoid mud, local people take bridleway that leaves from walled cemetery to cross field, through gate, and walk with stream and hedge on Right. Pass through next gate, and almost immediately over gate on Right. (Here, you leave official way but this solution is widely used.) Bear Left to ascend diagonally up field to stile in corner, and so onto road.**

Cross road, and up bank to pass through small gate. Turn Right and follow path along by wood. In about 400 yards *365 m*, through small gate to enter wood and continue with wood boundary on Left.

There are fine views through trees on your Right, across the Vale of Evesham.

Emerge from woods and proceed along field boundary with hedge on Left. At Starveall farm track and barn, continue ahead on little-used metalled road. In about ten minutes, at T junction, turn Right along road, and then turn Left along avenue to Mickleton Hills Farm.

Just before the farm buildings, in the vegetable garden on the Left, are very superior 'girl' scarecrows, the work of Mr Fred Keyte. Their hair is brass wire and bailing cord. On request he has moved them near to the hedge just so Footpath-Tourers can photograph them.

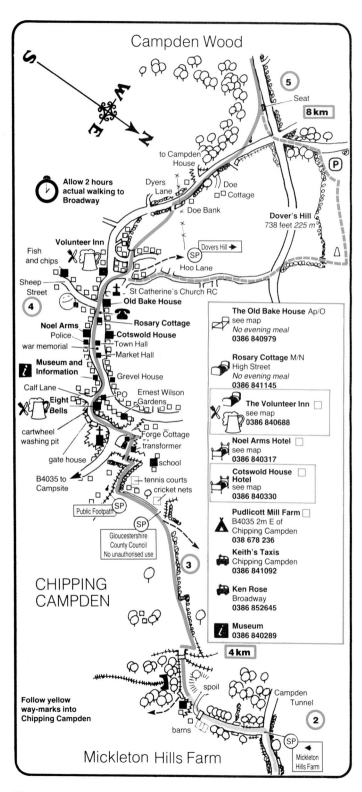

Campden Wood

⑤

Seat

8 km

to Campden House

Dyers Lane

Doe Cottage

Doe Bank

Dover's Hill
738 feet *225 m*

Dovers Hill →

Hoo Lane

Ⓟ

Allow 2 hours actual walking to Broadway

Volunteer Inn

Fish and chips

St Catherine's Church RC

Old Bake House

Sheep Street

④

Rosary Cottage

Noel Arms

Police

war memorial

Cotswold House

Town Hall

Market Hall

Museum and Information

Grevel House

Calf Lane

Eight Bells

Ernest Wilson Gardens

PO

cartwheel washing pit

Forge Cottage

transformer

gate house

school

B4035 to Campsite

tennis courts

cricket nets

Public Footpath   SP

SP

Gloucestershire County Council
No unauthorised use

③

CHIPPING CAMPDEN

4 km

spoil

Campden Tunnel

②

Follow yellow way-marks into Chipping Campden

barns

SP

Mickleton Hills Farm ←

Mickleton Hills Farm

The Old Bake House Ap/O
see map
No evening meal
0386 840979

Rosary Cottage M/N
High Street
No evening meal
0386 841145

The Volunteer Inn ☐
see map
0386 840688

Noel Arms Hotel ☐
see map
0386 840317

Cotswold House Hotel ☐
see map
0386 840330

Pudlicott Mill Farm ☐
B4035 2m E of
Chipping Campden
038 678 236

Keith's Taxis
Chipping Campden
0386 841092

Ken Rose
Broadway
0386 852645

Museum
0386 840289

Mickleton Hills Farm to Campden Wood

Going: An easy field walk into Chipping Campden, followed by a well-walked route up to Campden Wood.

Route passes in front of farm wall on Left and bears Right between spoil heap and copse over railway-tunnel entrance.

The tunnel on the Paddington–Worcester line, built in the 1850s, was the scene of a pitched battle when the great engineer, Isambard Kingdom Brunel, personally led a charge of 2,000 navvies, armed with picks and shovels, to drive off the navvies of an unwelcome rival contractor.

Over gate and stone foot-bridge; turn Right to corner of field, where turn Left and walk length of field with hedge on Right. At school playing fields, turn Left along ditch. At fence behind houses, turn Right along fenced path in front of school. Just after sharp Left turn, go over stile on Right, cross school drive, and along narrow, fenced path with transformer on Right. Bear Left in front of Forge Cottage onto road in Chipping Campden. Cross busy road to pass in front of church. Follow road round to Right to enter the broad High Street, where turn Left.

Chipping Campden is the finest of the Cotswold wool towns, with many attractive and historic stone buildings. Do not miss the opportunity to visit the beautiful church of St James, rebuilt in the fifteenth century when Campden was the centre of the rich wool trade. Many fine memorials include one to Lady Penelope Noel, who died from blood-poisoning after pricking her finger working with coloured silks. Note the priceless fifteenth-century alter hangings. In the room above the porch are displayed documents, records and occasional exhibitions. *Excellent guidebook.*

On leaving the churchyard, note on your Left the splendid lodges – once the gateway to the seventeenth-century manor house, burnt down by Royalists. Note the stone pediments on either side of the gateway – chimneys for the lodges. On your way to the High Street see on the Left the now dry cart-wheel wash. Opposite are attractive alms-houses built in 1612. Enter the High Street opposite Grevel House, which is an excellent example of fourteenth-century stonework. In Woolstaplers Hall are eleven rooms of fascinating exhibits, including an early balloon and an 1880 parachute. In the centre of the High Street is the Market Hall (1612). Now in the care of the National Trust, it narrowly escaped being shipped to the USA. *Recommended* 'Chipping Campden – Short History & Guide', *on sale at Bennett's Wine Store.*

Opposite Volunteer Inn, turn Right past Roman Catholic church of St Catherine. (Note yellow arrow and white disc way-marks of the Cotswold Way.) After about 150 yards *137 m,* at St Peter's Cottage, turn Left along metalled path running between back gardens. Cross over housing-estate road to continue along path which runs into field. At field entrance turn half Right to walk along path passing diagonally through crops to far corner of field. Here emerge onto Dyers Lane and turn Right.

After about five-minutes walking, at footpath sign on Left, take diagonal path through crops, which cuts off field corner, and continues along by road, below the road bank.

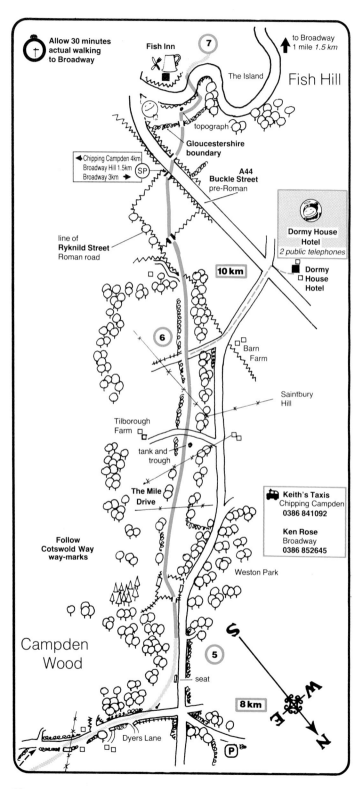

Allow 30 minutes actual walking to Broadway

Fish Inn

(7)

The Island

to Broadway 1 mile *1.5 km*

Fish Hill

topograph

Gloucestershire boundary

◄ Chipping Campden 4km
Broadway Hill 1.5km
Broadway 3km ►

(SP)

A44 Buckle Street pre-Roman

Dormy House Hotel
2 public telephones

Dormy House Hotel

line of Ryknild Street Roman road

10 km

(6)

Barn Farm

Saintbury Hill

Tilborough Farm

tank and trough

The Mile Drive

Keith's Taxis
Chipping Campden
0386 841092

Ken Rose
Broadway
0386 852645

Follow Cotswold Way way-marks

Weston Park

Campden Wood

(5)

seat

8 km

Dyers Lane

(P)

18

Campden Wood to Fish Hill

Going: A delightful, level walk along the grassy Mile Drive, finally crossing the route of a Roman road, and one considerably older.

Continue ahead, walking at foot of road embankment, until crossing stile into walled enclosure. Leave through gap diagonally Left, and continue with hedge on Left.

This broad, grassy way is the Mile Drive. Note that we have now briefly joined the route of the Cotswold Way, which runs for a hundred miles along the Cotswold escarpment from Chipping Campden to the city of Bath, and the yellow arrow and white disc way-marks will lead us into Broadway.

After crossing two farm tracks, Mile Drive tapers to end, and we leave it by gap in wall.

The wall continuing on your Left marks the line of the Roman Ryknield Street which ran from the Roman Fosse Way near Bourton-on-the-Water, and ran north-west to Wall in Staffordshire, then north-east to join Ermine Street near Doncaster.

Keeping same line of direction across two fields, cross stone stile onto ancient Buckle Street, which is now a busy motor road.

Buckle Street was a native pre-wheel, pre-Roman, high-level road running over the Wolds. We cross it twice more during our Footpath-Tour.

Leave road by stone stile almost opposite, cross corner of field, and over wall on Left into Fish Hill picnic area.

A topograph, the work of Winchcombe craftsmen, indicates the direction of places unseen – including New York!

In a short distance to the Right, follow the way-marks and cross the busy A44 Evesham/Moreton-in-Marsh road. To Left is Fish Inn.

The quaint building of the Fish was built in 1775 as a gazebo with a bowling-green for Farncombe House a mile away, and was very popular with gentlemen of leisure. It later became an ale house to revive travellers who had toiled up the hill from Broadway.

Nearby were gallows where two men and a woman were hanged in 1660 for the murder of Edward Harrison. Two years later the 'murdered' Harrison returned with a strange story of robbers, pirates, shipwrecks and slavery. Local people still refer to the tragic and bizarre affair as the Campden Wonder.

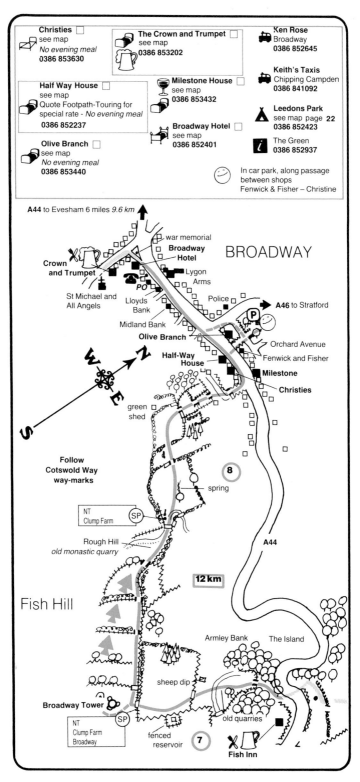

Christies ☐
see map
No evening meal
0386 853630

The Crown and Trumpet ☐
see map
0386 853202

Ken Rose
Broadway
0386 852645

Keith's Taxis
Chipping Campden
0386 841092

Half Way House ☐
see map
Quote Footpath-Touring for
special rate - *No evening meal*
0386 852237

Milestone House ☐
see map
0386 853432

Broadway Hotel ☐
see map
0386 852401

Leedons Park
see map page 22
0386 852423

Olive Branch ☐
see map
No evening meal
0386 853440

i The Green
0386 852937

In car park, along passage
between shops
Fenwick & Fisher – Christine

A44 to Evesham 6 miles *9.6 km*

war memorial
Broadway Hotel

BROADWAY

Crown and Trumpet

Lygon Arms

St Michael and All Angels

PO

Lloyds Bank

Police

A46 to Stratford

P

Midland Bank

Olive Branch

Orchard Avenue

Half-Way House

Fenwick and Fisher

Milestone

N W E S

Christies

green shed

Follow Cotswold Way way-marks

8

spring

NT Clump Farm SP

Rough Hill
old monastic quarry

A44

Fish Hill

12 km

Armley Bank

The Island

sheep dip

Broadway Tower

NT Clump Farm Broadway SP

fenced reservoir

old quarries

7

7

Fish Inn

Fish Hill to Broadway

Going: A short walk through the grassy mounds of old quarries leads to one of England's finest viewpoints. From there a well-walked field path leads easily down into Broadway.

Follow footpath signs into woods above Armley Bank, and emerge into grassed-over old quarry workings. Ahead see castellated top of Broadway Tower, and head for that along the hollows. Through gate with sheep-dip down on Right. Through gate at base of Tower.

The 55 foot *17 m* Broadway Tower was built at the end of the eighteenth century by the sixth Earl of Coventry on what was known as Beacon Hill at 1,031 feet *314 m*. Various reasons are put forward for the erection of this magnificent folly. One suggests that it was Lord Coventry's way of proving to his wife Peggy that the hill could indeed be seen from their estate at Croome Court, fifteen miles to the west! But like all good follies, it was certainly intended to be enjoyed. In 1827 a printing-press was installed here, and later it was leased to two Oxford tutors, who included amongst their guests the pre-Raphaelite painter, Sir Edward Burne-Jones, and William Morris, the great social reformer and designer. Today it houses various displays, allows you to produce your own souvenir, and, if you are lucky, allows you to see over twelve counties. Your knees will love the seventy-two steps! *Open April – Oct, 10a.m.–6p.m.*

With field boundaries on Right, drop down through fields, on obvious path. At group of gates, head down centre of field, with tree and spring on Right. Over stile, then through gap in hedge, and follow path which veers to Right to cross stile in corner of field. Fences, stiles and signposts now shepherd you into main street of Broadway. Turn Left.

Broadway was once an important overnight stopping place for the Welsh drovers on the way to Smithfield Market in London, with up to 200 head of cattle at a time. Now Broadway's wide, main street is busy with tourists.

But people have always been here. Pottery from 2000 BC and the Roman era has been discovered near the green. At one time the settlement belonged to the Benedictine Abbey of Pershore. In the seventeenth century this was an important overnight stop for stage-coach travellers, and fresh and extra horses were supplied for the climb up Fish Hill. (The daily Royal Mail coach would leave London at 7p.m. and travel via High Wycombe and Oxford to arrive at Broadway at 7.30a.m. next morning.)

There are many houses of interest and the high street must be one of the most photographed in England. The Lygon Arms, once the White Hart pub, claims to have been receiving guests before the reign of Henry VIII. The front doorway is fifteenth-century, and a four-poster bed bears the date 1620 – the year the Mayflower sailed for America.

The history of all the most interesting buildings, with many old, photographs are contained in A Walk about Broadway, *available from David Jelf's bookshop.*

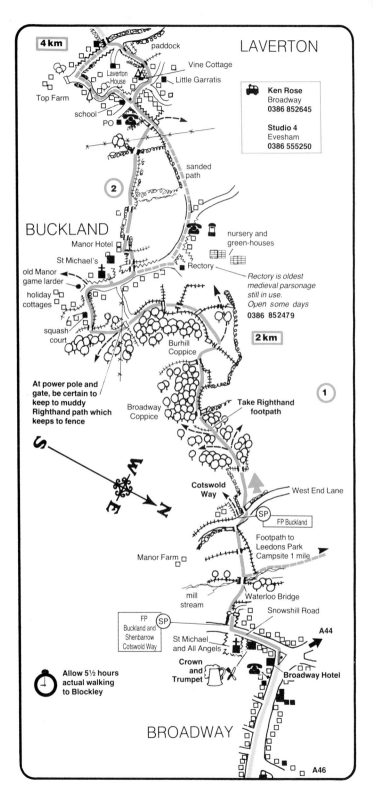

4 km

LAVERTON

paddock

Vine Cottage
Little Garratis
Laverton House
Top Farm
school
PO

sanded path

②

BUCKLAND

Manor Hotel
St Michael's
old Manor game larder
holiday cottages
squash court

Burhill Coppice

At power pole and gate, be certain to keep to muddy Righthand path which keeps to fence

Broadway Coppice

nursery and green-houses

Rectory

Rectory is oldest medieval parsonage still in use.
Open some days
0386 852479

2 km

①

Take Righthand footpath

Cotswold Way

West End Lane

SP FP Buckland

Footpath to Leedons Park Campsite 1 mile

Manor Farm

mill stream

Waterloo Bridge

Snowshill Road

A44

FP Buckland and Shenbarrow Cotswold Way SP

St Michael and All Angels

Crown and Trumpet

Broadway Hotel

Allow 5½ hours actual walking to Blockley

BROADWAY

A46

Ken Rose
Broadway
0386 852645

Studio 4
Evesham
0386 555250

22

Lunch: The Snowshill Arms in the village of Snowshill offers a good range of bar meals, and at 6 miles *10 km,* is conveniently situated almost exactly halfway through today's walk. Incidentally the excellent Mount Inn in Stanton (3½ miles *6 km*) is open for coffees, or bar drinks, weekdays from 10.30a.m., Sundays from 12 noon.

Broadway to Laverton

Going: The day begins with a steady climb of 160 feet *50 m* to Burhill Coppice, followed by a rapid descent into the delightful valley village of Buckland. An easy, level walk follows into Laverton.

Leave Broadway by village green, turning Left into Snowshill Road. Just beyond St Michael's 'new' church take drive on Right signposted 'Footpath to Buckland and Shenbarrow'. (Notice too the Cotswold Way way-marks.) Through kiss-gate at end of drive, and down field to cross mill-stream by splendidly named Waterloo Bridge. Continue ahead over stile in fence, and at stile in Right-hand corner of field cross lane to another stile. *(Important: Note that here we end our brief association with the Cotswold Way.)* Take footpath on Right signposted to Buckland. With hedge on Left, ascend steeply up field to enter Broadway Coppice ahead.

Follow main, often muddy, path through woods, and leave by stile, where fence on Right constricts you to walk closely along edge of coppice. At stile, emerge from woods into field and proceed to Right-hand tip of Burhill Coppice. Cross stile and, ignoring well-walked track ahead, bear Left up to coppice fence and follow this, bearing around to Left. Through two fences by gate and stile. At third fence, pass through small gate to enter woods, and continue, keeping fence on your Right. Look for stile on Right onto garden path down into Buckland, with group of holiday cottages on Left. Continue down to church.

Do make time to visit St Michael's church. Note the superb medieval painted roof with roses and devil's heads, and the seventeenth-century seating and oak wainscoting. There is an embroidered fifteenth-century velvet cope and a sixteenth-century bowl of maplewood and silver. The east window came from Hailes Abbey.

Just beyond entrance to Manor Hotel, take signposted footpath on Left. In few yards, stile on Left puts you into hotel grounds, but continue in same direction as before. There follows well-walked field path, which enters Laverton village by enclosed path. At crossroads, with tree and seat in centre, turn Right along village road. At fork, keep to Left, and almost immediately turn Left up signposted footpath by wall and two fir trees. With fence on Left, cross pony paddock with series of stiles, onto road. Turn left and in few yards, cross stile on Right onto signposted footpath.

For an alternative route showing some of Laverton's attractive cottages and gardens, keep straight ahead at the crossroads and follow road around to locate stile after the last house on the Left.

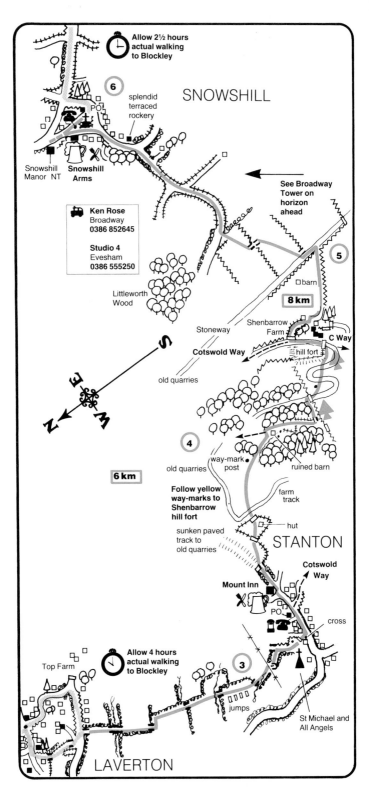

Allow 2½ hours actual walking to Blockley

⑥ splendid terraced rockery

SNOWSHILL

POL

Snowshill Manor NT **Snowshill Arms**

See Broadway Tower on horizon ahead

Ken Rose
Broadway
0386 852645

Studio 4
Evesham
0386 555250

⑤

□ barn

8 km

Littleworth Wood

Shenbarrow Farm

Stoneway

C Way

Cotswold Way

hill fort

old quarries

N / S / E / W compass

old quarries

④

way-mark post

ruined barn

6 km

farm track

Follow yellow way-marks to Shenbarrow hill fort

sunken paved track to old quarries

hut

STANTON

Cotswold Way

Mount Inn

PO

cross

Allow 4 hours actual walking to Blockley

Top Farm

③

jumps

St Michael and All Angels

LAVERTON

24

Laverton to Snowshill

Going: Pleasant field walk into the charming village of Stanton, followed by a most attractive climb (550 feet *170 m*) through parkland and woods, to the lofty platform of an Iron Age hill-fort. From there an easy walk down into Snowshill.

The field footpath is well walked and maintained. In fifth field, take care if horses are exercising over line of jumps by path. In next field, locate coy kiss-gate at entrance to hedged path leading into churchyard.

A visit to the church of St Michael and All Angels will enrich your tour if time permits. There are many features of interest including two pulpits, one fourteenth-century. *Useful guide book.*

Leave churchyard by short drive, and turn Left on main street of Stanton.

Note the wayside cross on the Right with a twelfth-century base. This is a quite beautiful village with buildings mainly sixteenth- to seventeenth-century. Restoration was largely due to the architect, Sir Philip Scott, who lived here 1906–1937.

Continue up street (ignoring Cotswold Way signs to Right), to Mount Inn. Behind inn, take sunken, hedged path, which climbs steeply up to gate and stile, known locally as Dirty Lane. Over stile, follow fence on Right to go through two gates in quick succession. Cross over farm track, and keeping same line of direction, head for nearest point of wood, where post way-mark indicates a track through trees. Follow track, with stream on Right, and follow way-marks turning you Left and Right to pass ruined barn. From barn proceed through trees with fence on Right, until gateway, when fence transfers to Left. Just before wall ahead, over stile on Left to scramble steeply up to farm track. Here, turn Right through gate, and continue to scramble up half Left to top of rise. Across hollow lies Shenbarrow Iron Age hill-fort. Descend to cross hairpin bend track at bottom of hollow, and back up to pass round to Right of fenced fort site.

The hill-fort was excavated in 1935, and finds, now in Gloucester museum, included pottery, and bone needles.

Through gate on Left to pass across fort plateau, in front of farm. At ditch and earth bank perimeter of fort, through gate on Right, and follow tree-filled ditch round through farm buildings. At end of buildings, turn Left up farm track with wall on Right. At top, turn Left on ancient Stoneway.

The importance of the quarries above the village – known before the Romans and last worked in 1910 – is reflected in the names Stanton (stone village) and Stanway (stone way).

In few yards, just beyond wall boundary on Right, turn half Right diagonally across field. Aim for clump of trees in distance until post way-mark at double stile is located. Continue same line to join lane where turn Right. Down to T junction with road and turn Left down into village of Snowshill.

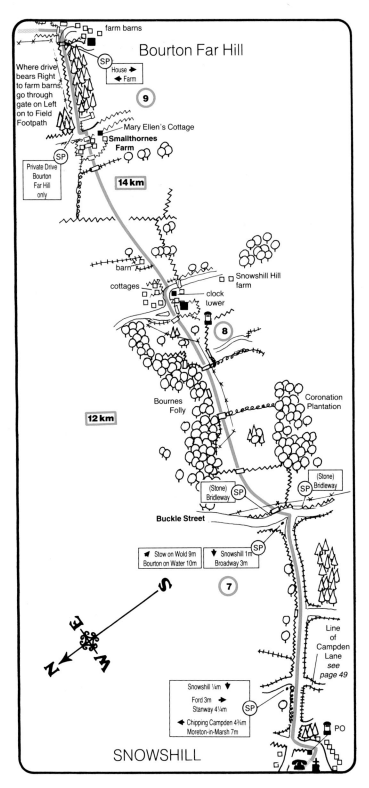

farm barns

Bourton Far Hill

SP

House →
← Farm

Where drive
bears Right
to farm barns,
go through
gate on Left
on to Field
Footpath

(9)

Mary Ellen's Cottage

SP

Smallthornes
Farm

14 km

Private Drive
Bourton
Far Hill
only

barn

cottages

Snowshill Hill
farm

clock
tower

(8)

Bournes
Folly

Coronation
Plantation

12 km

(Stone)
Bridleway

(Stone)
Bridleway

SP

SP

Buckle Street

◀ Stow on Wold 9m
Bourton on Water 10m

▼ Snowshill 1m
Broadway 3m

SP

(7)

Line
of
Campden
Lane
see
page 49

Snowshill ¼m ▼

Ford 3m ➤
Stanway 4¼m

SP

◀ Chipping Campden 4¾m
Moreton-in-Marsh 7m

PO

SNOWSHILL

Snowshill to Bourton Far Hill Farm

Going: A pleasant, straightforward walk. The first mile is along road, but this develops into a pleasant walk on a wide grass track, and continues along a private drive.

Snowshill is an attractive hillside village largely grouped round the church of St Barnabus. Neatly mown grass banks, colourful hanging flower baskets and typical Cotswold stone cottages tend to keep the photographers busy here. However the main attraction is the Manor House with its bizarre contents. Charles Paget Wade, craftsman and collector extraordinary, purchased the attractive Tudor manor house – once owned by Catherine Parr, wife of Henry VIII – in 1919 with family fortunes that came from sugar planting in the West Indies. He then proceeded to cram the rooms with his collection. In 1951 he presented the house and its contents to the National Trust, who preserve it more or less as he left it. Everything is there – somewhere. Camel trappings, Kurdistan rugs, Japanese Samurai armour, musical instruments, tools, toys, tins and pinned butterflies. In the entrance hall is the motto – *'Nequid Pereat'* – 'Let nothing perish'. Charles Wade remained true to that. Queen Mary once observed that he must have been even more remarkable than his hoarded treasures. You will only believe it if you see it. *Open April and Oct, Sat and Sun. May – end Sept, Wed to Sun, 11a.m.–1p.m. 2p.m.–6p.m.*

From Manor, with pub and church on Right, up road to turn Left by corner post office. Continue up road to leave village. At crossroad turn Right along Stow road. After about fifteen minutes come to road junction with wild remains of old quarry on Left. *Note that there is bridleway straight ahead, but turn Left on road.* In few yards on Right, by pole, through metal gate to join grass farm-track bridleway.

Continue fine walk, across three fields, with trees of Bournes Folly on Left. Track is obscure in paddock before Snowshill Hill farm, but head for gate at centre of group of buildings. Through gate onto road and continue ahead to follow private drive which passes between farm buildings. Drive bears to Right. At clocktower, turn Left off drive, with cottages on Left, to follow wide farm track across three fields. Through series of four gates to emerge onto road at Smallthornes farm. Turn Left and almost immediately turn Right onto Bourton Far Hill private drive.

Animal lovers will enjoy meeting the donkeys at Smallthornes.

Continue along drive with firs on Right. After about five-minutes walking, a drive to Bourton Far Hill house bears round to Right, but continue ahead through gate. Drive now immediately again bears to Right to farm buildings, but instead leave drive and turn Left through gate, to walk in field with wall on Left and horse-riding dressage enclosure on Right.

We again cross Ryknield Street, which we last saw near Chipping Campden, but its course is marked here only by a hedgerow.

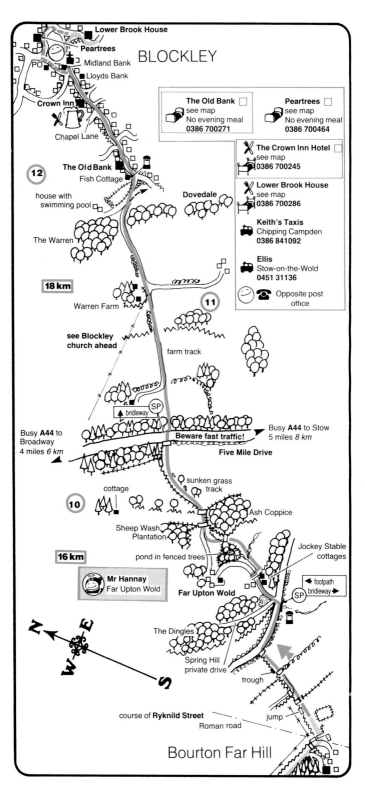

BLOCKLEY

Lower Brook House
Peartrees
Midland Bank
Lloyds Bank
PO
Crown Inn
Chapel Lane

The Old Bank
Fish Cottage

(12)

house with
swimming pool

Dovedale

The Warren

18 km

Warren Farm

see Blockley
church ahead

(11)

farm track

bridleway
SP

Busy **A44** to
Broadway
4 miles *6 km*

Beware fast traffic!

Busy **A44** to Stow
5 miles *8 km*

Five Mile Drive

sunken grass
track

cottage

(10)

Ash Coppice

Sheep Wash
Plantation

pond in fenced trees

16 km

Jockey Stable
cottages

footpath
bridleway

SP

Mr Hannay
Far Upton Wold

Far Upton Wold

The Dingles

N E W S

Spring Hill
private drive

trough

course of **Ryknild Street**
Roman road

jump

Bourton Far Hill

	The Old Bank ☐		Peartrees ☐
	see map		see map
	No evening meal		No evening meal
	0386 700271		0386 700464

The Crown Inn Hotel ☐
see map
0386 700245

Lower Brook House ☐
see map
0386 700286

Keith's Taxis
Chipping Campden
0386 841092

Ellis
Stow-on-the-Wold
0451 31136

☎ Opposite post
office

28

Bourton Far Hill to Blockley

Going: An attractive walk which requires a little attention to navigation for the first mile. Once over the busy A44 road, a farm track is soon reached which leads easily into the interesting village of Blockley.

Continue ahead along field footpath, with wall on Left. In third field, path drops steeply down to road, where turn Right. In 200 yards *180 m* turn Left into Far Upton Wold private drive.

Note the poetic 'no-litter' request.

By restored Jockey Stable cottages, cross cattle grid, and immediately turn Right along cottage garden wall for few paces, then Left to follow stream on Left. Continue along by stream to pond concealed by fenced copse. Through gate, and follow wall of Ash Coppice on Right. Note that stream emerges from this coppice so it is sensible to keep well to Left in wet conditions.

A faint, wide grass track is joined. Follow this through two field gates and up sunken, wide grass track which levels out before reaching A44 road. Cross this busy road with great care.

This stretch of the A44 is known as the Five Mile Drive.

Turn Right, and in few paces turn Left on bridleway through belt of trees to emerge onto field – usually cropped. Path continues straight ahead across middle of field to hedge opposite, where there is gap situated about equidistant between Right-hand copse, and Left-hand copse with barn. Continue ahead through gap onto farm track which leads past Warren Farm into trees of Warren Wood. At T junction, turn Left by Fish Cottage, into Blockley.

In the stream in front of Fish Cottage there once lived a pet trout. A wooden-framed stone plaque on the cottage wall below the balcony recalls this. It reads:

> *In Memory of the Old Fish*
> *Under the soil the Old Fish do lie*
> *Twenty years he lived and then did die*
> *He was so tame you understand*
> *He would come and eat out of your hand*
> Died April 20th 1885, Aged 20 years, At Fish Cottage.

In the centre of the village, take the Right fork at the Midland Bank to go through the churchyard.

Blockley is a village of dignified seventeenth- to nineteenth-century houses and attractively converted mill buildings, and it somehow manages to hide itself from tourists. It was once famed for its skills in taking cocoons of raw silk straight from China, and preparing and winding the silken thread onto wooden bobbins – two miles of filament from each cocoon – ready for the ribbon weavers of Coventry. *See* What to see in Historic Blockley, *on sale in the church of St Peter & St Paul.*

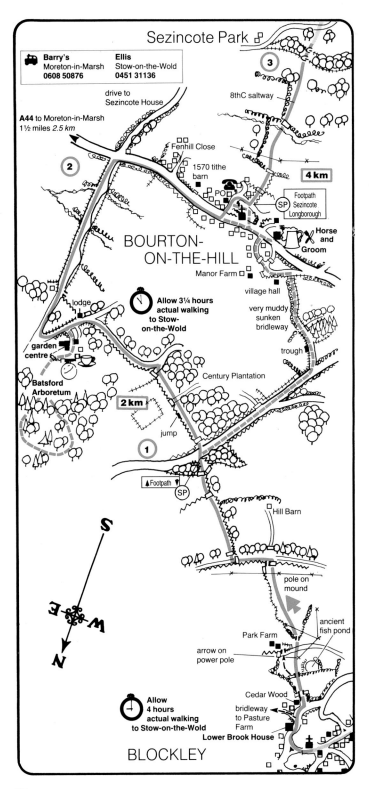

Sezincote Park

Barry's
Moreton-in-Marsh
0608 50876

Ellis
Stow-on-the-Wold
0451 31136

drive to
Sezincote House

8thC saltway

A44 to Moreton-in-Marsh
1½ miles *2.5 km*

③

Fenhill Close

4 km

1570 tithe
barn

PO

②

Footpath
SP Sezincote
Longborough

BOURTON-
ON-THE-HILL

**Horse
and
Groom**

Manor Farm

village hall

lodge

Allow 3¼ hours
actual walking
to Stow-
on-the-Wold

very muddy
sunken
bridleway

trough

**garden
centre**

Century Plantation

2 km

**Batsford
Arboretum**

jump

①

S

▲Footpath▼
SP

Hill Barn

pole on
mound

E

W

N

Park Farm

ancient
fish pond

arrow on
power pole

Cedar Wood

Allow
4 hours
actual walking
to Stow-on-the-Wold

bridleway ◄
to Pasture
Farm
Lower Brook House

BLOCKLEY

30

Lunch: There are two possible visits today that are well worth your consideration – Batsford Arboretum and Sezincote house and/or garden (Thurs & Fri only) – and two recommended pubs are conveniently positioned to provide lunch whatever schedule you decide upon. Horse & Groom at Bourton-on-the-Hill (2½ miles *4 km*); Fox Inn at Broadwell (6½ miles *10.5 km*).

Blockley to Sezincote

Going: The day begins with a fairly steep plod of nearly 400 feet *120 m* up to the road at Century Plantation. The route goes through the plantation to allow a recommended visit to the fascinating arboretum – botanical tree garden – at Batsford. (For those choosing to forego such delights, a shorter route into Bourton-on-the-Hill is given.) From the arboretum, there is a level lane and pavement walk leading easily into Bourton-on-the-Hill, followed by a pleasant field route into Sezincote Park.

From Blockley churchyard, turn Right onto main road. Continue past Lower Brook House Hotel on Left. Immediately past Cedar Wood cottage, turn Left up paved bridleway. Cross stile, and up field with hedge on Left. At next stile, half Right, note way-mark on pole between Park Farm and ancient, banked fish pond. Cross farm drive, and over stile in field corner. Up field, with battered fence on Left, toward prominent pole on mound.

Look back for a fine view over Blockley.

In Left corner of field, over stile, turn Left on tree-lined track. Through gate and immediately through hunting gate on Right. With wall on Right, across two fields, and through copse onto road. (For route avoiding arboretum, turn Right on road. Beyond Right fork, take muddy track on Left leading into Bourton village, where turn Left on road down to church.)

For arboretum, turn Right on road, and immediately turn Left through gate onto footpath along edge of wood, with high wall on Left. Footpath joins tree-lined farm drive, and continues with wall of Left. Through stone gate-posts by lodge, and second turn on Left into garden centre and arboretum. *Open daily April–Nov, 10a.m.–5p.m.*

The arboretum contains over 1,000 trees collected from all over the world and arranged in delightful and colourful settings, which include an enormous bronze Buddha, a stone Chinese lion, and a Japanese rest-house. *A guide book suggests a route and indicates some of the most important species.*

Leave gardens by far exit, and down road to join A44, where turn Right into Bourton-on-the-Hill. Turn Left down to post office/shop, or continue along A44 to go through churchyard.

St Laurence church has several items of interest including standard measures of a bushel and a peck dated 1816.

At rear of church, turn up walled footpath signposted Sezincote. Through three gates and two kiss-gates into park.

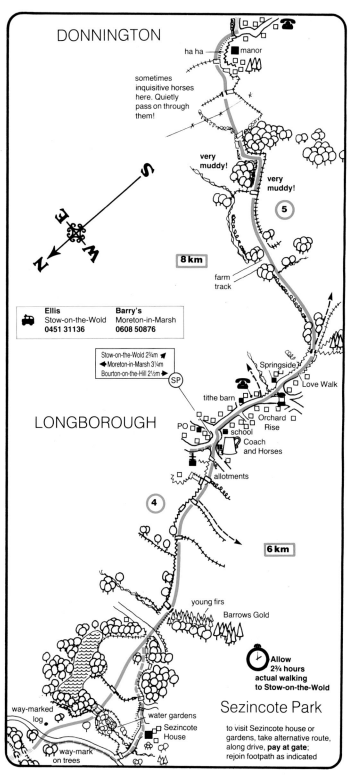

DONNINGTON

ha ha — manor

sometimes inquisitive horses here. Quietly pass on through them!

very muddy!

very muddy!

5

8 km

farm track

Ellis
Stow-on-the-Wold
0451 31136

Barry's
Moreton-in-Marsh
0608 50876

Stow-on-the-Wold 2¾m ➤
◄ Moreton-in-Marsh 3¼m
Bourton-on-the-Hill 2½m

SP

LONGBOROUGH

Springside

Love Walk

tithe barn

Orchard Rise

PO

school

Coach and Horses

allotments

4

6 km

young firs

Barrows Gold

Allow 2¾ hours actual walking to Stow-on-the-Wold

Sezincote Park

way-marked log

water gardens

Sezincote House

way-mark on trees

to visit Sezincote house or gardens, take alternative route, along drive, **pay at gate**; rejoin footpath as indicated

Sezincote Park to Donnington

Going: A pleasant walk across Sezincote Park, with an opportunity to visit the beautiful gardens and house, (Thurs & Fri only). A level, easy, ancient track then leads into Longborough. After the village, there is more parkland, but a section just before Donnington is much used by horse-riders, and consequently is usually very muddy.

From here to Stow-on-the-Wold our route follows an ancient salt road. *For more information on salt ways please see page 49.*

From two kiss gates and belt of trees, continue forward to Sezincote drive. Note way-mark on Right-hand clump of trees.

(To visit Sezincote house and gardens, turn Right along the drive, and after about five minutes turn Left through a signposted gate-way. *Pay for admission.* Rejoin the route by continuing along the drive in front of the house, cross a cattle grid, and go through the white gate into the park. Follow the fence on your Right to a walled gap in the trees, and the farm road. (See below**.)

Sezincote gardens are beautiful, with magnificent vistas, oriental water gardens and masses of colour. The house, with its Mogul architecture and onion-shaped dome is said to have been inspiration for Prince Regent when Brighton Pavilion was rebuilt. *Gardens open Jan – Nov, Thurs and Fri, 2p.m.–6p.m. House open May, June, July and Sept, Thurs and Fri, 2p.m.–6p.m.*

If you choose not to visit house and garden, cross drive and note way-mark on log on Left. Drop down to two gates between trees concealing ponds. Straight ahead through gate in fence. See Sezincote house over to Right.

Continue up to Right-hand corner of parkland, into walled gap in trees, through kiss-gate, and across farm road. With fence on Right, continue ahead to Barrows Gold young firs plantation and through kiss-gate. Straight ahead on wide grass track, with field boundaries now on Left. After allotments on Right, turn Left on road into Longborough.**

The church, down on the Left past the war memorial, once belonged to Hailes Abbey and contains some impressive tombs and a beautiful fourteenth-century font.

Bear Right past Coach and Horses pub, and again Right past the school, (signposted Stow). At end of village take Left fork, where stream tumbles beneath road. At end of Love Walk, over stone stile and follow track with hedge on Left.

In the thirteenth century this flat land was known as the 'saltemor'.

Continue same line across parkland, to join fence on Right which leads up to gate which leads into fenced muddy track along edge of wood. With relief, leave wood through gate, into field, and half Right up to stile and gate in corner of field. Over stile, passing quietly through sometimes inquisitive horses. Proceed with fence on Right, and continue round with ha-ha (trench) in front of Donnington Manor on Right, to gate and so onto village road.

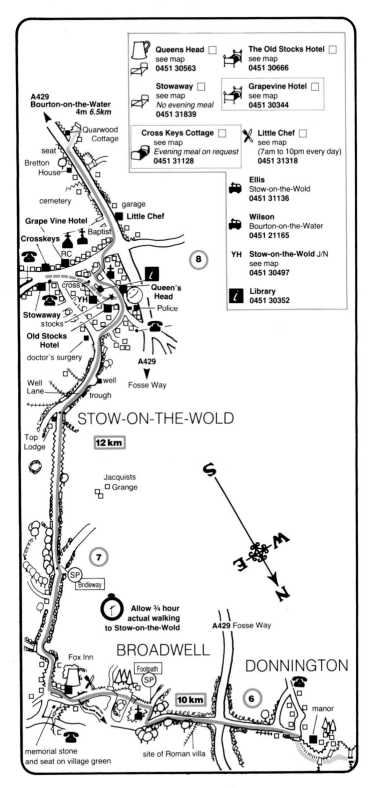

Queens Head ☐
see map
0451 30563

The Old Stocks Hotel ☐
see map
0451 30666

Stowaway ☐
see map
No evening meal
0451 31839

Grapevine Hotel ☐
see map
0451 30344

Cross Keys Cottage ☐
see map
Evening meal on request
0451 31128

Little Chef ☐
see map
(7am to 10pm every day)
0451 31318

Ellis
Stow-on-the-Wold
0451 31136

Wilson
Bourton-on-the-Water
0451 21165

YH Stow-on-the-Wold J/N
see map
0451 30497

Library
0451 30352

A429
Bourton-on-the-Water
4m 6.5km

Quarwood Cottage

seat
Bretton House

cemetery

garage

Grape Vine Hotel

Crosskeys

Little Chef

Baptist

RC

8

Queen's Head

Police

YH

cross

Stowaway

stocks

Old Stocks Hotel

doctor's surgery

Well Lane

well

trough

A429
Fosse Way

STOW-ON-THE-WOLD

12 km

Top Lodge

Jacquists
Grange

7

SP
Bridleway

Allow ¾ hour
actual walking
to Stow-on-the-Wold

A429 Fosse Way

BROADWELL

DONNINGTON

Fox Inn

Footpath
SP

10 km

6

manor

memorial stone
and seat on village green

site of Roman villa

34

Donnington to Stow-on-the-Wold

Going: A short road walk to Broadwell is followed by a pleasant walk on an ancient salt way into Stow-on-the-Wold.

Salt was an important commodity in the Saxon and medieval economy, and salt ways radiated from the salt-producing areas of Northwich and Droitwich. This section was much used in the eighth century and runs from Chipping Campden to the Thames at Bampton.

In 1645, Donnington was the scene of the last battle of the Civil War. On these fields men ran, horses galloped, men fought and died. Defeated Royalist troops, numbering 1,500, were imprisoned in Stow church, including their commander, Lord Astley, a tough soldier who had fought as a sergeant major in the Netherlands. He made this famous prayer the previous year before the battle of Newbury:

Lord I shall be verie busy this day; I may forget Thee but doe not thou forget me

Turn Left on road and head for Fosse Way, A429 (see page 41). Exercise great caution at the crossroad, and continue over to lane into Broadwell.

The first field on your Left was the site of a Roman villa.

At entrance to village, turn Right, and in few paces turn Left to take footpath through churchyard.

St Paul's church, (twelfth-century, restored 1860s) contains fine memorials, particularly kneeling Herbert Weston and wife.

Continue ahead to rejoin village road, and by Fox Inn on Right, opposite large village green, with boulder memorial.

The Fox Inn will sell you excellent Donnington ales, unusually good food, and *Broadwell – a Short History.*

Continue to end of green, turn Right up road signposted to Stow-on-the-Wold. After about ten minutes of gentle uphill road walking, turn Left into bridleway guarded by black-and-white post; after about another ten minutes, come to second black-and-white post, and turn Right into Well Lane.

The large stone well was the sole water supply for Stow. As recently as the nineteenth century there were always women and children carrying their yoke and buckets up the lane. Horse-drawn tuns carried water up to the square to sell it at a farthing a bucket.

Turn Right at Surgery, and follow road up into Stow-on-the-Wold.

Stow-on-the-Wold 'where the wind blows cold' sits at 750 feet *229 m* on a rounded hill at the junction of eight ancient routes. A Stone Age axe was found here, and the oval outlines of an Iron Age hill-fort can be traced. The Romans made use of an existing track when they built Fosse Way on the outskirts. During the great days of the wool trade the square was an important sheep market. It is now a busy tourist centre with more than its fair share of antique shops. There are stocks on the square. St Edward's church should be visited. A moving painting of the Crucifixion is by Gaspar de Craeyes (1582–1669). *Stow Chamber of Commerce has produced a good guidebook.*

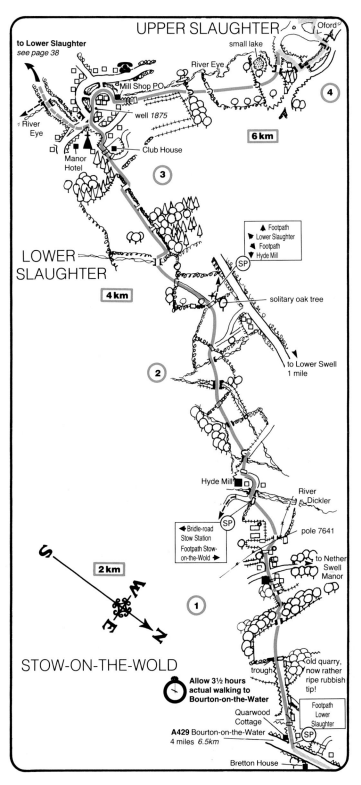

UPPER SLAUGHTER

Oford

to Lower Slaughter
see page 38

small lake

River Eye

Mill Shop PO

6 km

well *1875*

River
Eye

Club House

④

Manor
Hotel

③

▲ Footpath
▶ Lower Slaughter
  Footpath
▼ Hyde Mill

LOWER
SLAUGHTER

SP

4 km

solitary oak tree

to Lower Swell
1 mile

②

Hyde Mill

River
Dickler

SP

◀ Bridle-road
  Stow Station
  Footpath Stow-
  on-the-Wold ▶

pole 7641

to Nether
Swell
Manor

2 km

S

W

E

N

①

STOW-ON-THE-WOLD

old quarry,
now rather
ripe rubbish
tip!

trough

Allow 3½ hours
actual walking to
Bourton-on-the-Water

Footpath
Lower
Slaughter

Quarwood
Cottage

SP

A429 Bourton-on-the-Water
4 miles *6.5km*

Bretton House

Lunch: Bourton-on-the-Water – about 7 miles *11 km* – offers a wide lunch choice, from fish and chips to a three-star hotel restaurant. If you are brave you could treat yourself to a bar-lunch in the splendid Lords of the Manor, Upper Slaughter – mention Footpath-Touring and you will be made very welcome.

Stow-on-the-Wold to Upper Slaughter

Going: From hilltop Stow the route quickly drops down to the water meadows of the River Dickler. Now very easy – but often soggy – field walking to delightful Lower Slaughter; and pleasant walk by River Eye to Upper Slaughter.

For those in a hurry to get to Bourton-on-the-Water with its many 'attractions', an alternative, half-an-hour route from Lower Slaughter is indicated. This would allow a later completion of the five-mile circuit walk: Bourton – Lower Slaughter – Upper Slaughter – Buckle Street – Windrush Valley – Bourton. See map, page 38.

Leave Stow by turning Left on A429 Burford–Warwick road. Past cemetery on Left. A few yards beyond Bretton House, cross road with care to join signposted footpath along farm track by Quarwood Cottage. Track ends by old quarry on Right. Over stile into field, to drop down, very slightly Right, to locate stile giving entry to hillside trees. Follow path steeply down through trees and over stile, then, with field boundary on Left, pass through gates, and continue ahead through cottages and farm buildings of Nether Swell. Before last two large barns on Left, veer to Right to cross stile into field.

From stile, head half Left to white rails of bridge over River Dickler at Hyde Mill. Cross over bridge and follow road round to Left, and in few yards through gate on Right. Leave track at kiss-gate on Left, just over stream. Bear Left and cross field to stile at trees and stream. Through gate in hedge opposite, and cross two footbridges to gate in hedge on Right. From this gate, ignore farm tracks which head for farm buildings in far Right-hand corner, but head for gate by solitary oak tree. Through gate, follow track, (signposted Lower Slaughter), to pass through another gate, cross corner of next field to foot-bridge. This leads into large field, where follow Right-hand boundary. Just before fir trees at end of field, side-step Right to walk with boundary on Left. Pass clubhouse to emerge onto road by Lower Slaughter church, and turn Left.

There was a church here in 1235, but present St Mary's was rebuilt in 1867. However the glass-fibre tip to spire is new!

(For short route to Bourton, turn Left before road bridge. Opposite Manor Hotel, Right onto path leading to Coach & Horses pub, cross A429 to track between houses, and Left on Bourton road. Opposite council depot, take footpath Right, between school and games field to High Street, by church. See map page 38.)

Turn Right before road bridge for charming walk with River Eye on Left. Follow path round to mill and water wheel. Just past mill/post office, turn Left along walled passage. From two kiss-gates continue along bank with river on Left. Path now leaves river. Through third kiss-gate, above small lake on Left, drop down half-Left to locate footbridge in field corner, and up narrow path to road in Upper Slaughter.

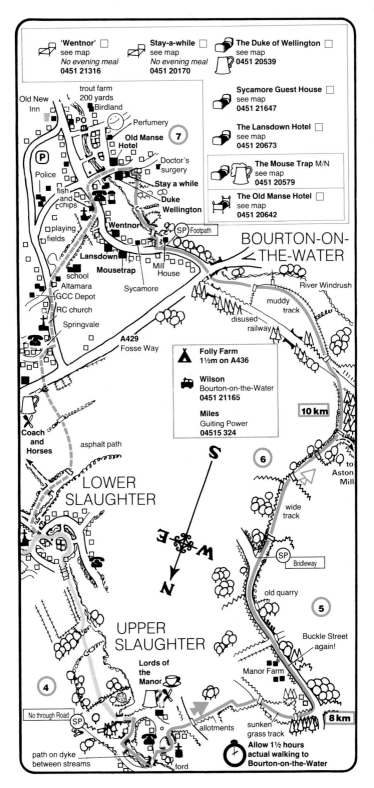

'Wentnor' ☐
see map
No evening meal
0451 21316

Stay-a-while ☐
see map
No evening meal
0451 20170

The Duke of Wellington ☐
see map
0451 20539

Sycamore Guest House ☐
see map
0451 21647

The Lansdown Hotel ☐
see map
0451 20673

The Mouse Trap M/N
see map
0451 20579

The Old Manse Hotel ☐
see map
0451 20642

Old New Inn

trout farm 200 yards

Birdland

PO

Perfumery

Old Manse Hotel

7

Doctor's surgery

P

Police

Stay a while

Duke Wellington

fish and chips

Wentnor

SP Footpath

playing fields

Lansdown

BOURTON-ON-THE-WATER

Mousetrap

Mill House

Sycamore

school

River Windrush

Altamara GCC Depot

muddy track

RC church

disused railway

Springvale

A429 Fosse Way

▲ Folly Farm
1½m on A436

🚐 Wilson
Bourton-on-the-Water
0451 21165

Miles
Guiting Power
04515 324

10 km

Coach and Horses

asphalt path

LOWER SLAUGHTER

6

to Aston Mill

wide track

S

E   W

N

SP Bridleway

old quarry

5

UPPER SLAUGHTER

Buckle Street again!

Manor Farm

Lords of the Manor

4

No through Road

SP

allotments

8 km

path on dyke between streams

ford

sunken grass track

⏱ Allow 1½ hours
actual walking to
Bourton-on-the-Water

Upper Slaughter to Bourton-on-the-Water

Going: A climb up to our old friend, the ridge route of Buckle Street, followed by an easy walk down to Windrush valley, and a pleasant, though in some places muddy, route into Bourton.

There are several versions of the origin of the gruesome name 'Slaughter', but it is probably nothing more than a corruption of the name 'de Soletres' who were lords of the manor in the reign of Henry II.

At road, turn Right to go down to white-railed bridge over young River Eye. Just over bridge turn Left along No Through Road, or more interesting route would be to locate path along top of dyke between two streams. At much-photographed footbridge and ford, turn Left up towards church, and after first house on Right, along passage into churchyard.

St Peter's church, originally Norman, was much rebuilt in the Middle Ages. See the fine tomb (1854) to Revd F. E. Witts, a famous diarist.

Leave churchyard by sunken path leading to pleasant village square with wall-enclosed trees in centre.

The eight attractive cottages on the square were remodelled in 1906 by Sir Edwin Lutyens. The Lords of the Manor hotel was once a rectory. Revd Witts's *Diary of a Cotswold Parson* is on sale here.

Turn Right off square up to Cheltenham road, cross, and through gate to ascend sunken track with wall and allotments on Right. Through gate on Right to follow sunken grass track around to join road (Buckle Street), where turn Left to pass in front of Manor Farm. After about ten-minutes walking, turn Right onto signposted bridleway. Follow this wide track down through two fields. Where track bears down Right to Aston Mill, turn Left through gate with firs on Right.

Join old Banbury–Cheltenham railway for few yards, then Right through gate to join muddy bridleway along Windrush river meadows, with fence on Right. Leave river meadows at bridge to cross over busy A429 road.

Follow willows on Right. At Mill House turn Right onto very attractive riverside path into Bourton-on-the-Water.

The pleasing, wide main street, with its low stone bridges over the River Windrush, has long been popular with tourists and consequently the town is full of 'attractions'. Oldest of these is the famous model village – an exact replica of Bourton to 1/9th scale – behind the sixteenth-century New Inn. The Motor Museum and Village Life Museum housed in the old mill is a fascinating collection of yesterday's vehicles, including several classics, hundreds of old advertising signs and much else. Charles Wade would have approved. The Model Railway boasts of over 400 sq ft of model scenery and moving trains. Birdland has 600 species of birds from penguins to flamingoes. The Perfumery exhibition is tastefully arranged and explains why you should buy their perfumes. Before the tourists came, there was an Iron Age settlement here (Salmonsbury), followed later by the Roman Second Augusta Legion. The cupola-topped church of St Lawrence has foundations from 709, a crypt of 1120, a 1328 chancel, and Victorian Gothic nave!

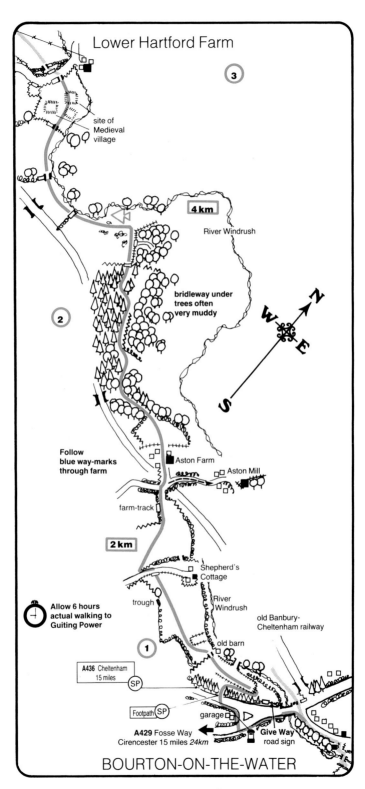

Lower Hartford Farm

③

site of
Medieval
village

4 km

River Windrush

N
W · E
S

bridleway under
trees often
very muddy

②

Follow
blue way-marks
through farm

Aston Farm

Aston Mill

farm-track

2 km

Shepherd's
Cottage

Allow 6 hours
actual walking to
Guiting Power

trough

River
Windrush

old Banbury-
Cheltenham railway

①

old barn

A436 Cheltenham
15 miles
SP

Footpath SP

garage

A429 Fosse Way
Cirencester 15 miles 24km

Give Way
road sign

BOURTON-ON-THE-WATER

Lunch: The friendly Black Horse Inn at Naunton – 2½ miles *4 km* – offers a very good range of bar meals. Refreshments are also usually available at the Cotswold Farm Park – 9 miles *14.5 km*.

Bourton to Lower Hartford Farm

Going: A pleasant walk along the water meadows of the River Windrush, with an interlude on the often muddy – and in places steep – bridleway running through the wood beyond Aston Farm.

Leave Bourton-on-the-Water along by River Windrush – the way that you entered – to bridge on Fosse Way.

The Fosse Way runs for 182 miles *290 km* from Ilchester, Somerset, to Lincoln and it is said that nowhere does it deviate more than 6 miles *10 km* from a dead straight line in its whole length. It gets its name from the *'foss'* or ditch which was built alongside the road as a temporary frontier when the Romans completed the occupation of Southern England approximately four years after the invasion. The handsome bridge bears a plaque to the Roman Second Legion, which surveyed and constructed this section.

Turn Left to cross bridge, and in few yards, cross busy A429 to 'Give Way' road sign. Turn Right through gate in hedge, at fence ahead turn Right to stile and cross into field. In far Right corner, over stile by derelict barn, and up Left to pass by fenced paddock on Right. Leave field by gate in fence ahead, onto farm road and turn Left for few paces. At end of wall turn Right to cross usually cropped field to join farm track at corner jutting into field. Drop down to join farm road sunken between high banks.

Turn Right on road, and in few yards turn Left to follow blue way-marks through Aston Farm. Clear of farm, cross field to enter wood at blue way-mark. Follow main bridleway which contorts muddily through wood to emerge at gate into field, and follow fence on Right. Where fence turns sharp Right, take track on Left which drops steeply down through gorse to join again the River Windrush. Through gate and stiles, keeping meandering river on Right. After grassy mounds of lost medieval village of Lower Hartford, through gate in wall, onto Lower Hartford Farm road.

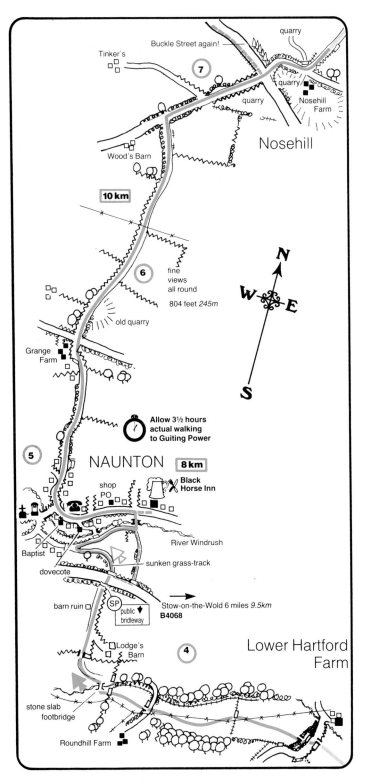

quarry

Buckle Street again!

Tinker's

7

quarry

quarry

Nosehill
Farm

Nosehill

Wood's Barn

10 km

6

fine
views
all round

804 feet *245m*

old quarry

Grange
Farm

⏱ **Allow 3½ hours
actual walking
to Guiting Power**

5

NAUNTON   **8 km**

🍺 **Black
Horse Inn**

shop
PO

✝

Baptist

River Windrush

sunken grass-track

dovecote

barn ruin

SP
public ▼
bridleway

➡ Stow-on-the-Wold 6 miles *9.5km*
B4068

Lodge's
Barn

4

Lower Hartford
Farm

stone slab
footbridge

Roundhill Farm

N
W E
S

Lower Hartford Farm to Nosehill

Going: Easy walking to join a farm track which climbs up to the
Gloucester–Stow ridge road, followed by a very pleasant descent
down a sunken, grass track to the village of Naunton, which
snuggles comfortably in its valley. A lane walk up and out of the
village leads to an airy farm track which, at nearly 800 feet *240 m*,
gives splendid views all round.

**Cross Lower Hartford Farm road to enter field. Footpath
follows power line. At end of second field, cross Roundhill Farm
track, and over stile to walk across field with fence and stream
on Right. At gate and stone-slab foot-bridge join farm track
which climbs up half Right, over stile, and proceed along track,
with wall on Right to B4068 road. Cross with care and through
gate opposite to follow sunken grass track down into valley.
At bottom, turn Right to walk along by our old friend, River
Windrush. At second bridge on Left, cross into main street of
charming village of Naunton.**

The Black Horse Inn lies a few paces to the Right. A former rector of
Naunton was a friend of Charles Dodgson (Lewis Carroll) and I have
been assured that part of *Alice in Wonderland* was written in the
rectory garden. Two miles to the east is Eyford Park where, beside a
well, in the seventeenth century, John Milton is said to have written
part of his epic poem *Paradise Lost*.

**Leave Naunton in direction of post office/shop and
church. Before church, follow road round to Right.**

Opposite the village hall is a seventeenth-century four-gabled
dovecote, with niches for 1,000 birds, which once belonged to the
manor house. In the Middle Ages only the lord of the manor was
permitted to keep doves for the benefit of the larder, which seems a
little unfair to those villagers on whose crops they fed!

St Andrew's church has a carved stone pulpit dated 1400 and an
attractive and colourful collection of embroidered hassocks. Among
the memorials is one to Dr William Oldys, 'barbarously murthered
by ye Rebells in ye yeare 1645', and also to his son Ambrose, who
died in 1710 'with better fortune'.

**Continue up lane, and over crossroads by Grange Farm.
Continue along track with wall on Left. After about fifteen
minutes of exposed walking, join lane and turn Right to cross
main road – Buckle Street again! Continue along lane with
quarries either side. Opposite Nosehill Farm, turn Left along
quarry track.**

Limestone in the Guiting area is quarried in freestone blocks
weighing up to six tons. Good quality stone is cream to buff in
colour, weathering to deep orange. It is extensively used in the
restoration of ecclesiastical and ancient buildings throughout the
Cotswolds and Midlands. Cotswold stone has been used in many
notable buildings, including St Paul's, Blenheim Palace and the
Oxford colleges. There is a story that Cotswold stone, used as
ballast on shipping to Australia, was collected and used in building
Sydney Cathedral!

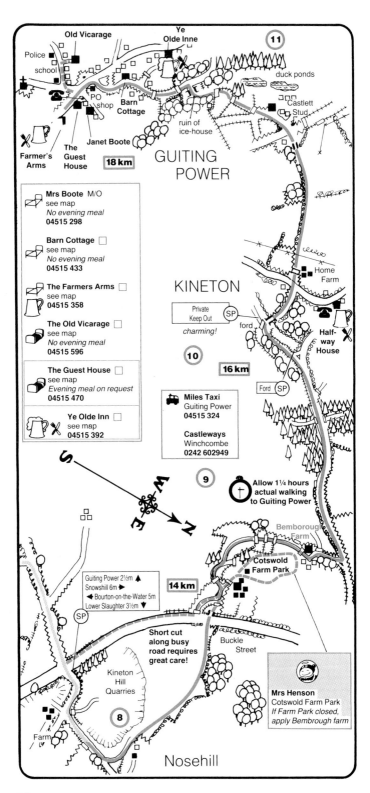

Old Vicarage

Ye Olde Inne

⑪

Police

school

duck ponds

PO shop

Barn Cottage

Castlett Stud

ruin of ice-house

Janet Boote

GUITING POWER

Farmer's Arms

The Guest House

18 km

Home Farm

🛏 **Mrs Boote** M/O
see map
No evening meal
04515 298

🛏 **Barn Cottage** ☐
see map
No evening meal
04515 433

🛏 **The Farmers Arms** ☐
see map
04515 358

KINETON

🛏 **The Old Vicarage** ☐
see map
No evening meal
04515 596

Private
Keep Out SP

charming!

ford

Half-way House

⑩

16 km

🛏 **The Guest House** ☐
see map
Evening meal on request
04515 470

🍺 **Ye Olde Inn** ☐
🍴 see map
04515 392

Ford SP

🚕 **Miles Taxi**
Guiting Power
04515 324

Castleways
Winchcombe
0242 602949

S

W ✦ N

E

⑨

⏱ **Allow 1¼ hours
actual walking
to Guiting Power**

Bemborough Farm

**Cotswold
Farm Park**

Guiting Power 2½m ▲
Snowshill 6m ▶
◀ Bourton-on-the-Water 5m
Lower Slaughter 3½m ▼

14 km

SP

**Short cut
along busy
road requires
great care!**

Buckle
Street

Kineton
Hill
Quarries

⑧

Farm

Mrs Henson
Cotswold Farm Park
*If Farm Park closed,
apply Bembrough farm*

Nosehill

Nosehill to Guiting Power

Going: Walking to the Cotswold Farm Park by way of the Kineton Hill quarries is half a mile further, and a great deal safer when traffic is heavy, than taking the more direct route along the road. From the Farm Park the route goes easily down a lane to cross the ford at Kineton, followed by the pleasant field and woodland walk which leads into the attractive village of Guiting Power.

Follow quarry track as it bears Left to pass in front of cottage on Right. Take care when quarry vehicles are working. Continue ahead on footpath which roughly follows field boundaries on Right. Cross Buckle Street again, and over stile to follow footpath right-of-way which runs through Cotswold Farm Park.

The park contains a unique collection of rare breeds of British farm animals, and is associated with the Rare Breeds Survival Trust. See the odd-looking small brown Soay sheep, unchanged since their domestication by Stone Age man, the black multi-horned sheep from St Kilda, Cotswold Lions, Norfolk Horns, Manx Loghtans, and sheep from the Orkneys. Look out for the bristly prehistoric pigs with their striped piglets. Fascinating. There are refreshments and a shop selling locally made craft items. *The footpath runs through the grounds, but to see the exhibits properly you will need to pay admission.* SHOW YOUR FOOTPATH-TOURING GUIDE TO GET A 10 PER CENT DISCOUNT. *Open May –end Sept, 10.30a.m.–6p.m. daily.*

Continue on footpath to pass through Bemborough Farm. At T junction, turn Left down lane. After about ten minutes easy walking take Left fork, and over pack-horse bridge by ford. Ascend lane to road.

A few yards to the Right is the Half-Way House pub.

Cross road slightly Left to follow footpath through Home Farm and across two fields, with boundaries on Left.

On the hill side in the distance, half Right, is Guiting Wood through which our route takes us tomorrow.

At end of field, over stile tucked into hedge corner, and through small cottage garden onto lane. Cross lane into splendid gateway of Castlett Stud Farm, and follow drive as it bears Left in front of farm buildings. Leave farmyard by small gate, and continue with fence on Left and through second small gate. Continue with fence now on Right – note extensive duck ponds down in valley on Right – and through small gate onto path which drops down through wood. At bottom, cross small foot-bridge over stream.

Until 1900, the three-storey Castlett Mill stood here. Only the collapsed ice-house or old dairy in the bank remains. The old name *catta slaed* meant 'valley of the wild cats'!

Over footbridge turn Left to ascend path, which leaves wood and becomes lane leading into Guiting Power.

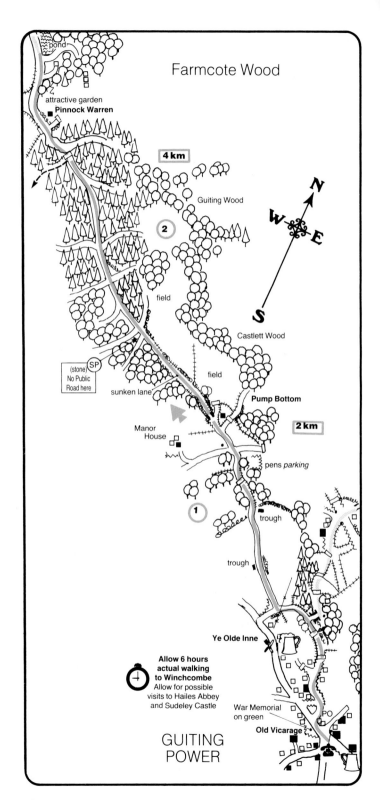

Farmcote Wood

pond

attractive garden
Pinnock Warren

4 km

Guiting Wood

2

field

Castlett Wood

(stone) SP
No Public
Road here

field

sunken lane

Pump Bottom

Manor
House

2 km

pens *parking*

1

trough

trough

Ye Olde Inne

**Allow 6 hours
actual walking
to Winchcombe**
Allow for possible
visits to Hailes Abbey
and Sudeley Castle

War Memorial
on green

PO

Old Vicarage

GUITING
POWER

Lunch: Today you will need to carry a packed lunch with you from Guiting Power. Probably the best place for a picnic might be after 6 miles *9.5 km* at the end of the wall just beyond Stumps Cross, with a superb view looking down Coscombe, and over to the 960 foot *293 m* Bredon Hill nearly ten miles away to the north-west. (A one mile detour from Didbrook, by footpath along by the railway, will take you to the A438/A46 roundabout with its busy pub, but this adds an hour's walking to your 12½-mile *20-km* day. The Bakery café at Stanway amusingly closes at lunchtime!)

Guiting Power to Farmcote Wood

Going: After retracing your steps out of Guiting Power, an easy walk along an unfenced farm road joins an ancient route that passes through Guiting Wood. A relaxing section which requires little navigation.

Guiting Power is another attractive, well-ordered village of soft Cotswold stone, with a neat village green, a village war-memorial cross, a flower-decorated post office, and the smell of freshly baked bread from the bakehouse. It gets its name from the Anglo-Saxon *gyte* – a 'torrent' – and Guiting was the old name for the River Windrush. The *le Poer* family owned property in the thirteenth century – hence Power. (Nearby is Temple Guiting, owned by the Knights Templar in the twelfth century.) There are two good pubs; the village once boasted of eight. The Old Bell inn is now The Guest House which will sell you a copy of *Guiting Power – A guide and history.* St Michael's church has two Norman doorways – one now blocked. The pulpit is carved in stone from Normandy. Every July the village organises an eight-day music and arts Festival.

Leave village green and, just past post office, turn Right to return along lane which brought you into Guiting Power. Continue back down into wood, but ignore footbridge on Right and ascend path ahead which bears round to Left. Opposite buildings, turn Right along unfenced farm road. After about ten-minutes walking, over crossroads, (car parking on Right), and continue to cottage at Pump Bottom.

From here water was once pumped up to the manor house on the Left.

To Left of cottage, locate stile to sunken and often overgrown path which rises up into Guiting Wood.

Where this rather trying path levels out to a good forestry track, note the old stone pillar on your Left.

Through wood, maintain same direction, ignoring all other tracks, and after about twenty minutes, leave wood through gate, and on road continue in same direction. Pass on Right cottage of Pinnock Warren, with small stream in front and attractive garden. At Farmcote Wood, stream becomes long pond on Right of road.

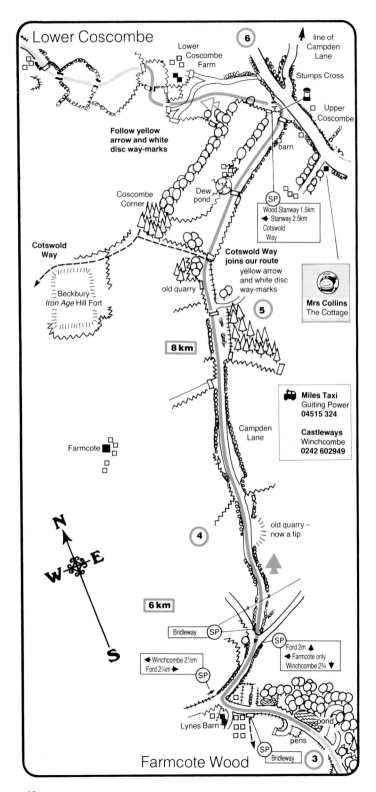

Lower Coscombe

line of
Campden
Lane

Lower
Coscombe
Farm

Stumps Cross

6

Upper
Coscombe

barn

**Follow yellow
arrow and white
disc way-marks**

Dew
pond

SP

Coscombe
Corner

Wood Stanway 1.5km
◄ Stanway 2.5km
Cotswold
Way

**Cotswold
Way**

**Cotswold Way
joins our route**

yellow arrow
and white disc
way-marks

Beckbury
Iron Age Hill Fort

old quarry

5

Mrs Collins
The Cottage

8 km

🚖 **Miles Taxi**
Guiting Power
04515 324

Campden
Lane

Castleways
Winchcombe
0242 602949

Farmcote

N

old quarry –
now a tip

4

W E

S

6 km

Bridleway SP

SP Ford 2m

◄ Winchcombe 2½m
Ford 2¼m

SP

◄ Farmcote only
Winchcombe 2¾ ▼

pond

Lynes Barn

pens

SP
Bridleway

3

Farmcote Wood

48

Farmcote Wood to Lower Coscombe

Going: Along a lane and an ancient highway to climb steadily 220 feet *67 m,* to a high point of 900 feet *274 m.* Easy walking follows to Stumps Cross with its splendid prospect down Coscombe, and a rapid descent.

Continue along road by pond. Past second, smaller pond to T junction at Lynes Barn, where turn Right. At fork, take bridleway which goes up between two roads.

This track between high hedges and walls is the old Campden lane, which runs to Chipping Campden from the old White Way, an ancient salt route (hence the 'white') and once the main Cirencester–Chipping Campden road. Salt was a vital commodity in ancient times, serving both as a medicine and a preservative. In the Middle Ages it acquired a social significance – at table the gentry sat 'above the salt', and lesser mortals below it. Roman soldiers were given an allowance to buy salt, the *salarium* – hence 'salary', and we still speak of someone as being 'not worth his salt'.

Salters Hill – 892 feet *272 m* – on another major salt route, the Salt Way, where we will be later today, can be seen a mile to the west, over Farmcote valley.

Continue to climb. Beyond old quarry, now ugly rubbish tip, track levels out, to make easy walking. At old quarry/ rubbish tip on the Left, now mercifully hidden by firs, the Cotswold Way with its yellow arrow and white disc markers joins our route to Wood Stanway (1½ miles *2.5 km).*

About 500 yards *460 m* to the Left can be seen the raised ramparts of Beckbury Iron Age hill-fort.

At the group of barns on the Left, see the remains of the old Dew pond where four walls meet in the centre. Despite popular belief, the name 'dew' has nothing to do with early morning moisture, but commemorates Mr Dew, a famous pond-builder in the Windsor area. He originated the formula which related circumference, depth, annual rainfall, and evaporation rate to ensure a permanently full pond. The barn of corrugated sheets is mounted on 'staddle stones' designed to keep vermin from stored grain.

At Stumps Cross go through gate to main road, and immediately turn Left to cross signposted stile.

Stumps Cross is just what it says, a stump of a long vanished cross standing close by the wall and stile.

With wall on Left, follow track with fine views down Coscombe. Where wall ends, continue downhill following yellow and white disc markers. By wall at Lower Coscombe Farm go over high stile; bear Right to cross stile in fence, and bear Left to go through gate.

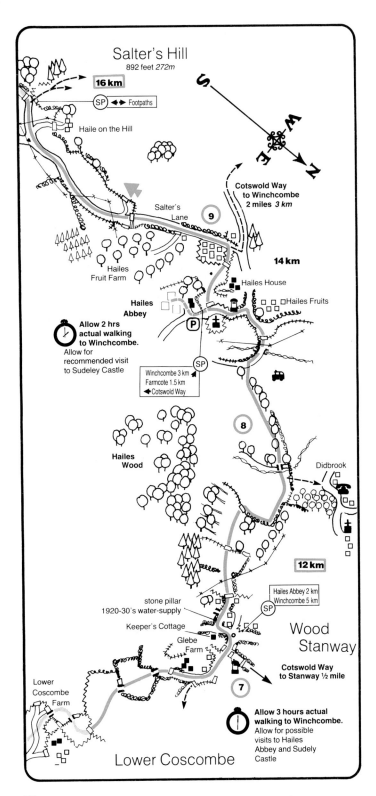

Salter's Hill
892 feet *272m*

16 km

SP ◄► Footpaths

Haile on the Hill

Salter's
Lane

⑨

Cotswold Way
to Winchcombe
2 miles *3 km*

14 km

Hailes House

Hailes
Abbey

Hailes Fruits

Allow 2 hrs
actual walking
to Winchcombe.
Allow for
recommended visit
to Sudeley Castle

P

SP

Winchcombe 3 km
Farmcote 1.5 km
◄ Cotswold Way

Hailes
Fruit Farm

⑧

Hailes
Wood

Didbrook

12 km

stone pillar
1920-30's water-supply

Hailes Abbey 2 km
Winchcombe 5 km

SP

Keeper's Cottage

Glebe
Farm

Wood
Stanway

Lower
Coscombe
Farm

Cotswold Way
to Stanway ½ mile

⑦

Allow 3 hours actual
walking to Winchcombe.
Allow for possible
visits to Hailes
Abbey and Sudely
Castle

Lower Coscombe

Lower Coscombe to Salter's Hill

Going: Continuation of field descent to hamlet of Wood Stanway. From here it is a pleasant, level field walk to historic Hailes Abbey. Take advantage of this restful site before beginning the steady plod up the steep Salt Way to Salter's Hill at 892 feet *272 m* – a climb of 540 feet *165 m.*

From Lower Coscombe Farm continue to follow yellow and white disc markers down through two fields to join lane at Glebe Farm into Wood Stanway.

Here the Cotswold Way markers exit Right on the path to Stanway, half a mile. Stanway has a famous 'St George and dragon' war memorial and a splendid seventeenth-century gatehouse to Stanway House. In the churchyard of St Peter's lies the remains of the notorious Dr Robert Dover, who was said to dose his patients with mercury, and, as a privateer, was said to have been captain of the ship which rescued Alexander Selkirk, the original Robinson Crusoe.

At road junction (fenced tree 'island'), turn Left along lane, and almost immediately – opposite Keeper's Cottage – turn Right. At lane end, through gate into field, and continue along level path at foot of rising ground on Left. Through second gate, turn Right to follow field boundary into corner, past orchard and path to Didbrook on Right. Over stile into next field and follow field boundary on Right which changes from hedge to line of trees.

At farm track turn Right, through gate and onto road, turn Left. First turn Left brings you to Hailes Abbey.

Hailes Abbey was founded in 1246 by Richard, younger brother of Henry III, for the Cistercian 'white monks', in thanksgiving for an escape from a shipwreck. In 1270 the abbey received a phial of 'Christ's blood'. A magnificent shrine was built to house this relic, and Hailes became one of the main pilgrimage centres in western England. This relic was later discredited and declared to be 'an unctuous gum'. On Christmas Eve 1539, the abbey was the victim of Henry VIII's famous Dissolution of the Monasteries. Plate and ornaments were taken, and lead stripped from the roof. Stone from the abbey was later incorporated in various buildings in the area. Only parts of the cloisters and foundations remain and are owned by the National Trust. However it is beautifully maintained, and there is an excellent museum of carved stone bosses, floor tiles, and other items which chronicle the fascinating story of this historic site.

Opposite the abbey is the still-standing church built 100 years before the abbey. It miraculously contains medieval stained glass rescued from the abbey, and some thirteenth-century wall paintings.

Opposite car park and church, through small gate to cross field between abbey and Hailes House.

Wall enclosed path emerges onto road, where turn Left to begin long ascent to Salter's Hill. It is a long pull so take it easy and enjoy the views.

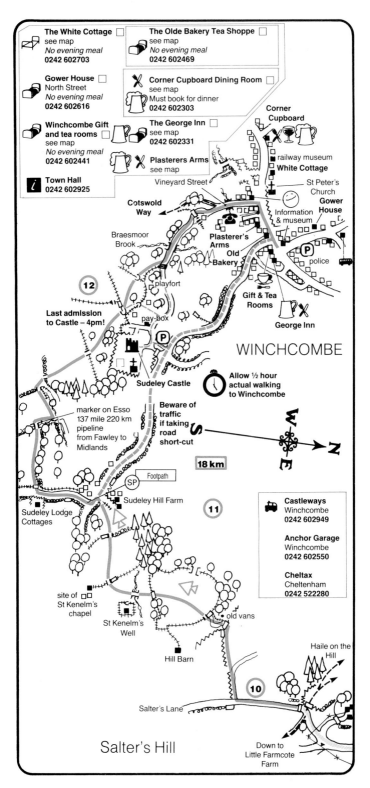

The White Cottage ☐
see map
No evening meal
0242 602703

The Olde Bakery Tea Shoppe ☐
see map
No evening meal
0242 602469

Gower House ☐
North Street
No evening meal
0242 602616

Corner Cupboard Dining Room ☐
see map
Must book for dinner
0242 602303

Winchcombe Gift and tea rooms ☐
see map
No evening meal
0242 602441

The George Inn ☐
see map
0242 602331

Plasterers Arms
see map

ℹ **Town Hall**
0242 602925

Corner Cupboard

railway museum
White Cottage

St Peter's Church

Gower House

Information & museum

Vineyard Street

Cotswold Way

Braesmoor Brook

Plasterer's Arms

Old Bakery

P police

playfort

Last admission to Castle – 4pm!

pay-box

Gift & Tea Rooms

P

WINCHCOMBE

Sudeley Castle

George Inn

Allow ½ hour actual walking to Winchcombe

Beware of traffic if taking road short-cut

marker on Esso 137 mile 220 km pipeline from Fawley to Midlands

N W S E

18 km

Footpath

SP

Sudeley Hill Farm

11

Sudeley Lodge Cottages

Castleways
Winchcombe
0242 602949

Anchor Garage
Winchcombe
0242 602550

Cheltax
Cheltenham
0242 522280

site of St Kenelm's chapel

St Kenelm's Well

old vans

Hill Barn

Haile on the Hill

10

Salter's Lane

Down to Little Farmcote Farm

Salter's Hill

Salter's Hill to Winchcombe

Going: Down hill all the way to Winchcombe, with the opportunity to make a recommended visit to Sudeley Castle.

Near summit of Salter's Hill, pass through gate across road and then at first field boundary wall on Right, take farm track to walk with wall on Left. At end of field, Left through second of two gates, and down to gate with fence and old vans on Right. Walk in direction of holy well building in next field ahead, passing through gate in hedge and over bridge in field.

In 811, Kenulf, King of Mercia, founded Winchcombe Abbey. After his death, legend says that his seven-year-old son, Kenelm, was murdered by his sister in Clent. By order of the Pope, the boy's body was carried by stages to Winchcombe. The night before the burial it rested on this hill, and a spring with healing powers appeared. A chapel to St Kenelm was the result. When 100 years later Emma Dent provided Winchcombe with a water supply from the spring, the spot was marked by this 'holy well'.

Cross over stile in fence, just below house on site of old St Kenelm chapel. Over next stile and drop down to road at Sudeley Hill Farm. Turn Left on road, and in few yards turn Right down No Through Road. Opposite Sudeley Lodge Cottages turn Right through small gate, to follow hedge on Right down to field corner. Over stile by Esso pipe-line marker, turn Right for few yards, then Left to follow down field with ditch on Right. Cross stile in corner, and over stile in hedge on Right. Up diagonally across field to cross stile in centre of fence. Now in Sudeley Castle Home Park, head for clump of trees by far corner of castle boundary wall, and through kiss-gate.

If you intend to make much-recommended diversion to visit castle, follow fence on Right and through kiss-gate to pass through children's play area to Portacabin ticket office ahead on drive.

There have been castles here since King Ethelred the Unready, and the site has witnessed a number of important historical events. Queen Catherine Parr, sixth wife and widow of Henry VIII, lived and died here. The tragic Lady Jane Grey was here. Queen Elizabeth I lived here as a child, and three times returned as queen. During the Civil War, King Charles I was here, and when the castle fell Oliver Cromwell ordered it to be 'slighted'. If you have time and energy do please include this in your tour. *Refreshments. Open: April–Oct. Grounds, 11a.m.–5.30p.m. House, noon–5p.m. From May–Aug, there are falconry displays, Sun, Tue, Wed, and Thur.*

Continue with castle boundary fence on right, and through kiss-gate. Continue with fence on Right to join castle drive by ornate iron gateposts, where turn Left along drive. Over bridge and on to West Lodge. Note that footpath passes through central arch of Lodge, but there is also small gate by drive cattle grid. Drive becomes Vineyard Street into Winchcombe.

Attractive Vineyard Street was once Duck Street, not because of ducks on Beesmoor Brook, but because by the bridge was the village ducking stool, where 'refractory' wives were punished!

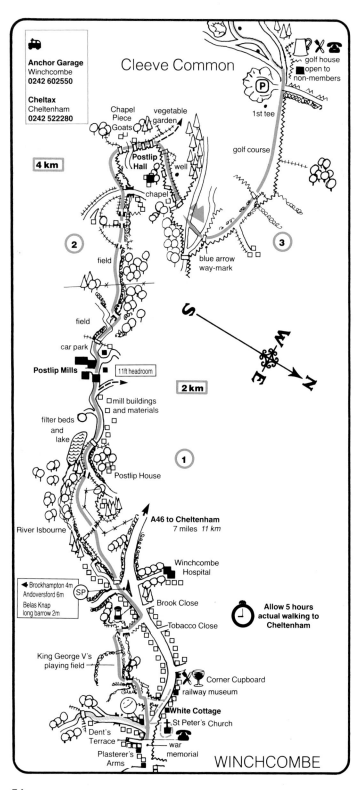

Anchor Garage
Winchcombe
0242 602550

Cheltax
Cheltenham
0242 522280

Cleeve Common

golf house
open to
non-members

1st tee

Chapel
Piece
Goats

vegetable
garden

golf course

4 km

Postlip
Hall

well

chapel

2

field

blue arrow
way-mark

3

field

S

car park

Postlip Mills

11ft headroom

2 km

W

mill buildings
and materials

E

filter beds
and
lake

1

Postlip House

River Isbourne

A46 to Cheltenham
7 miles 11 km

Brockhampton 4m
Andoversford 6m

Belas Knap
long barrow 2m

SP

Winchcombe
Hospital

Brook Close

Allow 5 hours
actual walking to
Cheltenham

Tobacco Close

King George V's
playing field

Corner Cupboard
railway museum

White Cottage
St Peter's Church

Dent's
Terrace

war
memorial

Plasterer's
Arms

WINCHCOMBE

Lunch: Cleeve Common Golf Club (3½ miles *6 km*) welcomes
Footpath-Touring customers. Licensed, with a range of bar
meals. Apart from the bar, there are also tables in the open and
under the veranda roof.

Winchcombe to Cleeve Common

Going: An ascent of 600 feet *180 m;* at first gently along by the
River Isbourne, getting steeper up on the common.

In the ninth century Winchcombe was an important administrative
centre of the kingdom of Mercia. In 969 the abbey founded by
Kenulf adopted Benedictine rule and, with the tomb of St Kenelm,
brought trade and visitors to the town. The town was walled and
had many of the street names which are still in use. The George Inn
still has the stone bath used by pilgrims under the gallery staircase
in the tiny courtyard. When Henry VIII dissolved the abbey the town
suffered, and in 1575 was obliged to petition Queen Elizabeth I, who
granted charters for a market and annual fair.

The 1853 town hall houses the Information Office, and a good folk
museum. An exhibition of international police memorabilia was
assembled over twenty-two years by M. Simms. *Open March–Oct,
10a.m.–4p.m. (not Sundays).* Note the stocks outside with, believe
it or not, seven leg holes. The fascinating Railway Museum in no
way confines itself to railway items; souvenirs and relics are on
sale. *Open daily 1p.m.–6p.m.* The much-photographed Dent
alms-houses (1865) were designed by Sir Gilbert Scott. Wesley
House (now a restaurant) is sixteenth-century.

**Leave Winchcombe opposite St Peter's church, along
path between Jacobean House and Chandos Alms-Houses.**

Be sure to visit the beautiful church, famous for its forty gargoyles
and alter cloth thought to be the work of Catherine of Aragon. In the
chancel is the tomb of Thomas Williams; space was left in the niche
for a statue of his wife, but she remarried and was buried else-
where. *Buy the excellent guide book to locate famous Imp carving,
and bullet holes made when Parliamentary troops shot Royalist
prisoners.*

**Continue on path, which twists into playing field, hedge
and river on Right. Kiss-gate and footbridge on Right lead up to
A46 between Brook Close and Tobacco Close. Turn Left, and
take Left minor fork opposite hospital, through gate in field
corner, proceed along bottom of field with hedge on Left. Leave
third field by stile in corner, down onto lane and continue in
same direction between lake, filter beds, cottages and buildings
of Postlip Mills (at one point beneath building with only 11 foot
headroom!). Leave mills by gate at far end of car park.**

There has been a paper mill here since 1719; it now exports filter
papers world-wide.

**From gate, few yards along rough track, but continue
ahead where it turns Left through hedge. Almost immediately
Left over stone footbridge into field, and turn Right along
hedge. Over three stiles, along narrow fenced path, over farm
road, and continue with high wall of Postlip Hall on Right. Follow
wall around three sides of Hall grounds; through gate onto
common.**

**Continue up wide track, through gate in wall (blue way-
mark), continue along clear track, wall on Right, to golf house.**

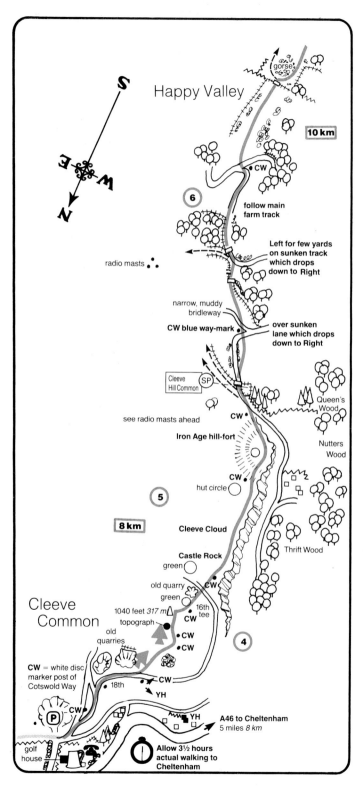

Happy Valley

gorse

10 km

6

follow main
farm track

CW

Left for few yards
on sunken track
which drops
down to Right

radio masts

narrow, muddy
bridleway

over sunken
lane which drops
down to Right

CW blue way-mark

Cleeve
Hill Common SP

Queen's
Wood

see radio masts ahead

CW

Iron Age hill-fort

Nutters
Wood

CW

hut circle

5

Cleeve Cloud

8 km

Thrift Wood

Castle Rock

green

old quarry
green

CW

Cleeve
Common

1040 feet 317 m

topograph

16th
tee

CW

4

old
quarries

CW

CW

CW = white disc
marker post of
Cotswold Way

CW

18th

YH

P

CW

YH

A46 to Cheltenham
5 miles 8 km

golf
house

Allow 3½ hours
actual walking to
Cheltenham

Cleeve Common to Happy Valley

Going: A fine walk on the common up to the 1040 foot *317 m* trig. point, and along the edge of the escarpment, with superb views over Cheltenham to the Black Mountains of Herefordshire.

Leave golf house by wide track, with car park in quarry on Left. In few yards take Right fork. *(For the length of this map our route coincides with the Cotswold Way, which is well marked by white and black stubby posts, bearing the white disc way-mark.)* Bear Right below two old quarries, and leave track (note path down Right to youth hostel), to climb up steeply Left to topograph and trig. point, avoiding golfers!

The topograph was erected at this popular viewpoint by the Rotary Club to mark its 1971 Golden Jubilee.

From trig. point drop down to Right following Cotswold Way markers by sixteenth tee on Right and past green and old quarry on Left. Cross track and proceed to cliff edge at Castle Rock.

This cliff-face is very popular with local rock climbers.

Continue with cliff edge on Right, along top of Cleeve Cloud, to earth banks and ditches of hill-fort.

Hill-forts were built in great numbers from the seventh century BC over most of England, and are early examples of military engineering and tribal organisation. Here, two banks with a ditch along each enclose about two acres. It was usual for those ditch-faces which confronted attackers to be built up with masonry or timber. Entrance gaps were the weak points and various designs attempted to solve this problem. Here, however, the access seems to have been limited to around the cliff ends of the earthworks. The name comes from Old English *clif* and *clud* – 'cliff' and 'rock'. Nutters Wood refers to the nutters who gathered nuts!

At far side of hill-fort, join track that comes up from Thrift Wood, and continue with wall on Right to gate and information board at entrance to common. Through gate take indistinct footpath alongside hedged track on Left. Where hedged track turns down Right as sunken lane, continue across, and immediately also across second track. Along narrow, often muddy bridleway with fence on Right. Through gate, so fence now on Left. Turn Left on sunken track for few yards and through gate on Right, to continue with fence and wood on Left.

When wood ends continue to follow main farm track. At T junction, leave wide track to go ahead and proceed along floor of Happy Valley.

This strange dry valley is the result of a lateral fault.

At end of 'valley', through gate in fence, into gorse-filled field and follow vague track that wanders round to Right, with fence on Right.

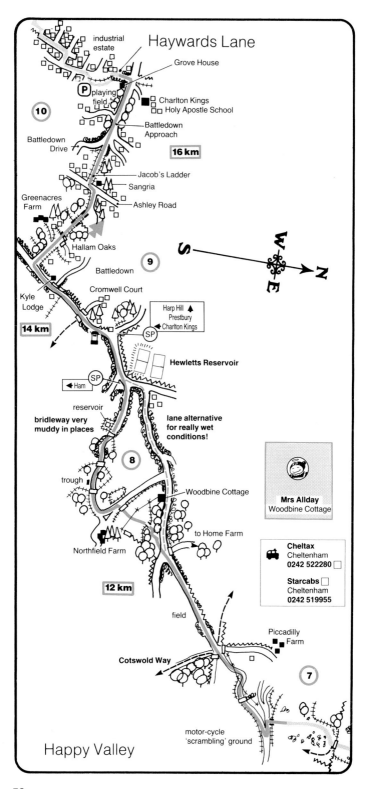

Haywards Lane

industrial estate

Grove House

P playing field

10

Charlton Kings
Holy Apostle School

Battledown Approach

Battledown Drive

16 km

Jacob's Ladder

Sangria

Greenacres Farm

Ashley Road

Hallam Oaks

Battledown

9

Cromwell Court

Kyle Lodge

Harp Hill ▲
Prestbury
◄ Charlton Kings

SP

14 km

SP

◄ Ham

reservoir

bridleway very muddy in places

lane alternative for really wet conditions!

8

trough

Woodbine Cottage

to Home Farm

Northfield Farm

12 km

Mrs Allday
Woodbine Cottage

Cheltax
Cheltenham
0242 522280 ☐

Starcabs ☐
Cheltenham
0242 519955

field

Piccadilly Farm

Cotswold Way

7

motor-cycle 'scrambling' ground

Happy Valley

Happy Valley to Hayward's Lane

Going: Apart from a small rise by Greenfield Farm to the top of Jacob's Ladder, this is an easy downhill route, beginning with muddy paths, and ending along the pavements of Cheltenham.

At far end of gorse-filled field, cross stile, and turn Left along fence into old quarry, now a motor-cyclists' playground. In few muddy yards, turn acutely Right on track to follow fence on Left. Continue down this sunken track to leave old quarry by gate, and down unfenced lane to Piccadilly Farm crossroads. *(Note that Cotswold Way walkers go off to Left.)* Over crossroads along lane which is hedged only on Right. At Home Farm crossroads, turn into woods on Left, wary of traffic coming down from Left. Follow way-marked path through wood, and over stile into field. Drop down through trees on bank and continue down field to gate and onto Northfield Farm lane. Instantly take Right fork, and turn Right onto bridleway.

This bridleway is pleasant enough although quite muddy in some places. In really wet conditions you may prefer to continue down the lane from Home Farm crossroads, to rejoin the route by Hewletts Reservoir.

From bridleway, turn Left on road, and continue with reservoir high wall on Right. Fork Left, signposted Charlton Kings. Beyond *Kyle Lodge* turn Right up drive to Greenacres Farm. Where drive bears Left continue ahead up field with fence on Right. Over stiles into claustrophobic passage between fences, fir trees and very private houses, and emerge onto Ashley Road. Half Left across road, and to Left of house, *Sangria*, join Jacob's Ladder fenced path which drops down to join Battledown Approach avenue.

The OS 1:50 000 map shows Battledown Hill as a hatched circle. The site of a hill-fort? Was a famous battle fought here? Cheltenham reference library says, 'No, just a hill.' Pity.

Continue down Battledown Approach. Opposite Charlton Kings Holy Apostle School, turn Left into Haywards Lane.

Until the beginning of the eighteenth century Cheltenham was a small market town described as 'near Winchcombe'. However, in 1718 a saline spring was discovered, and a Captain Henry Skillicorne built a spa to make available the medicinal benefits of the waters. The fortune of Cheltenham was assured when George III visited to take the waters with his family in 1788. The Duke of Wellington, who found that the waters cured his liver complaint, opened Assembly Rooms in the town. In 1825, the self-made MP, Joseph Pitt – who began his career by 'holding gentlemen's horses for a penny' – suggested the construction of a splendid pump room as the centre of his proposed Pittville estate. The stone-laying ceremony was a great day for Cheltenham, with a masonic procession, pealing bells and firing cannons. However, when the rooms were finally opened five years later the ceremony was not attended by Pitt, who was already disillusioned by the project, and was having considerable financial problems. But today the pump room still stands and you are free to taste the health-giving waters.

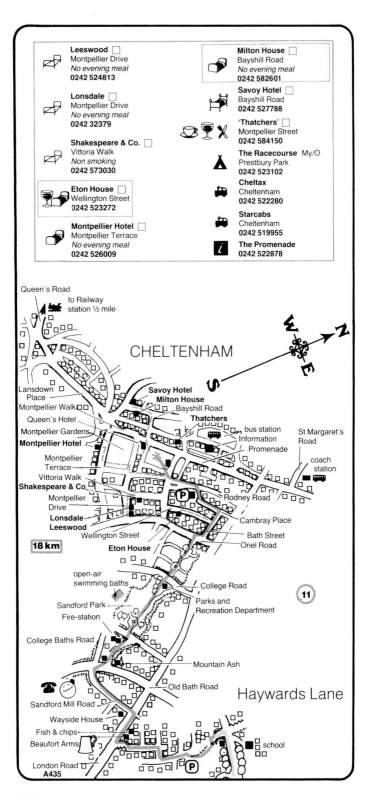

Leeswood ☐
Montpellier Drive
No evening meal
0242 524813

Lonsdale ☐
Montpellier Drive
No evening meal
0242 32379

Shakespeare & Co. ☐
Vittoria Walk
Non smoking
0242 573030

Eton House ☐
Wellington Street
0242 523272

Montpellier Hotel ☐
Montpellier Terrace
No evening meal
0242 526009

Milton House ☐
Bayshill Road
No evening meal
0242 582601

Savoy Hotel ☐
Bayshill Road
0242 527788

'Thatchers' ☐
Montpellier Street
0242 584150

The Racecourse My/O
Prestbury Park
0242 523102

Cheltax
Cheltenham
0242 522280

Starcabs
Cheltenham
0242 519955

The Promenade
0242 522878

Queen's Road

to Railway
station ½ mile

CHELTENHAM

Lansdown
Place
Montpellier Walk
Queen's Hotel
Montpellier Gardens
Montpellier Hotel

Montpellier
Terrace
Vittoria Walk
Shakespeare & Co.
Montpellier
Drive
Lonsdale
Leeswood
Wellington Street

18 km

Eton House

open-air
swimming baths

Sandford Park
Fire-station

College Baths Road

Sandford Mill Road

Wayside House
Fish & chips
Beaufort Arms

London Road
A435

Savoy Hotel
Milton House
Bayshill Road
Thatchers
bus station
Information
Promenade

St Margaret's
Road

coach
station

Rodney Road

Cambray Place

Bath Street
Oriel Road

College Road

Parks and
Recreation Department

(11)

Mountain Ash

Old Bath Road

Haywards Lane

school

Hayward's Lane to Imperial Gardens, Cheltenham

Going: The route has been chosen to get you into the centre of Cheltenham with a minimum of pavement walking. But when crossing roads please remember that you are now back in traffic, where everyone is on desperately urgent business!

You can avoid part of litter-decorated lane by stepping Left into children's playground area and walking along edge of playing field, returning to lane through car-park. Haywards Lane becomes residential Haywards Road. Turn Right into Rosehill Street, and immediately Left into Coltham Road. Traffic sign says 'cul-de-sac', but there is escape passage at end. Emerge from passage onto A435 London Road, and turn Right by Beaufort Arms pub. Take first turn on Left, Sandford Mill Road. At Bath Road, cross over half Right to locate path between office building and house, *Mountain Ash*.

On your Right is the young River Chelt, which crosses the town to join the River Severn 8 miles *13 km* to the north-west.

With fire-station on Left, over Keynsham Road into Sandford Park. Ahead through park to College Road, with park office in trees on Right, cross over into continuation of gardens.

Cheltenham is justly proud of its parks and its floral displays. There are several thousand spring bulbs in the various parks and beds throughout the town, and every June 100,000 bedding plants are added. The town also claims to have forty miles of avenues.

Ahead through water gardens onto busy Oriel Road. Cross with care, turn Right, then Left into Bath Street. At T junction of Cambray Place turn Left to find path to Right of Cambray Court at end. Turn Left on Rodney Road, along short dual-carriageway, and cross again Oriel Road. Turn Right towards Town Hall, behind which are Imperial Gardens. Well done, you have made it! You deserve a good hotel and a celebratory meal – I wish I could join you!

The Town Hall is now a splendid concert venue, and the municipal offices are today housed in a magnificent Regency terrace, once private houses on the Promenade.

No visit to the town is complete without visiting Montpellier Walk, where the shops are spaced with female figures used as columns, and based on the statues of Athens' Acropolis. The splendid Rotunda (1825), now Lloyds Bank, was once another pump room serving the waters. Nearby Barclays Bank was once a museum where geological specimens were on sale. A very recent addition is the new shopping courtyard. At the other end of the Promenade is the Regent Arcade, opened by HRH Princess Anne, which has a remarkable clock where a duck lays a golden egg every thirty seconds, a mouse appears at any one of ten doors, and a twelve-foot-long fish lights up and blows bubbles!

For details of Cheltenham museums – *see page 63.*

The Cotswolds and Wool

Millions of years ago, enormous pressures pushed up the sea bed to form a band of limestone which crosses England like a sash, beginning at the cliffs of Dorset, and passing up across to the Yorkshire Moors. North-east of the Severn estuary this limestone was raised and tilted, and the Cotswold hills were formed. Today a steep escarpment on the western edge gradually slopes down in the east towards the Thames valley, and in between are the valleys, rivers, rolling hills and woods that make this area such a distinctive part of the British landscape.

Prehistoric people farmed here, and Stone Age barrows mark ancient burial grounds; Iron Age hill-forts were built on lofty sites and their outlines are still traceable; the Romans came to build their great frontier road, the Fosse Way, and the remains of magnificent villas show where and how they lived. But it was in the thirteenth to the sixteenth centuries that the Cotswolds – with its wool industry – played such an important part in the country's history.

The spinning and weaving of wool was known in pre-Roman times, and the special characteristics of Cotswold wool made it the best in Europe. Over 5,000 tons a year left Britain in the fourteenth century. This was a time of exceedingly wealthy wool and cloth merchants – the most famous being the Cotswold merchant, Dick Whittington, who three times became Lord Mayor of London. Great houses were built and churches found generous benefactors. But imports of foreign wool, cotton and the explosion of the steam-powered northern industries helped to bring about the inevitable changes that always occur despite plans and protests. Today the great wool age is largely remembered by its achievements in stone – the honey-coloured Cotswold stone which is the hallmark of the soft charm and dignity of this most beautiful part of Britain.

Stratford-upon-Avon

Although not generally regarded as being in the Cotswolds, Stratford nevertheless makes an interesting start for this Footpath-Tour. The town acquired an enormous tourist industry as a consequence of William Shakespeare, who was born, educated and owned a house here. Throughout the year, pilgrims from all over the world can be seen at their devotions, especially on the Saturday nearest to 23 April – St George's Day and the bard's traditional birthday. There are many fine eighteenth-century houses and attractive half-timbered buildings.

The Shakespeare Centre: Built on site next to Birthplace to mark 400th anniversary; houses library, bookshop and occasional exhibitions. *Open Mon – Fri 9.30a.m.–5p.m. Sat – mornings only.*

Shakespeare's Birthplace: Fine half-timbered house where poet was born. Exhibits illustrate his life and history of property. Well presented. *Open daily 9.am.–6p.m. Sun 10a.m.–6p.m.*

Nash's House and New Place: Handsome timbered building with ground floor furnished in period style, and upstairs display illustrating town's history. Adjoining are Elizabethan Knott garden and foundations of New Place, large house which Shakespeare bought in 1597, and where he died on his fifty-second birthday. Unfortunately, house was pulled down in 1759 by Revd Francis Gastrell after tiff with Council. *Open daily 9a.m.–6p.m. (closed Sun).*

Stratford-upon-Avon

Hall's Croft: Shakespeare's daughter Susanna, wife of Dr John Hall, lived here. Now furnished in Elizabethan style, with one room fascinatingly equipped as seventeenth-century dispensary. *Open daily 9a.m.–6p.m. (closed Sun).*
INCLUSIVE TICKETS AVAILABLE FOR ALL ABOVE.

Tourist Information Office: Housed in timbered building, once town prison, later home of Shakespeare's daughter, Judith. *Ask for free street map.*

Grammar School: Fifteenth-century building where Shakespeare was pupil. Not open to public.

Swan Theatre, and Royal Shakespeare Theatre: Museum and Gallery: Strongly recommended daily backstage tours. Must book. For details telephone: 0789 296655.

Royal Shakespeare Theatre: Programme and bookings, telephone 0789 295623.

Harvard House: Elaborately carved overhanging floors (1596). Home of mother of John Harvard, founder of American University. *Open daily, April to Oct. 9a.m.–6p.m. Sun – afternoons only.*

Church of Holy Trinity: Beautiful church which warrants visit. Original north and south transepts built about 1210. *(Enter porch beneath recent work by my stone-mason son!)* Shakespeare's tomb and bust are in chancel. Fine stained glass windows and memorials. *Church book-shop offers various guides and histories.*

Cheltenham museums

May I recommend a further walk – about half-hour – which will introduce you to two delightful museums. First collect your free street map from the Tourist Information office *(see map).*

The Gustav Holst Birthplace Museum: Clarence Road, Pittville. The ground floor of this Regency house contains a fascinating collection of items associated with the composer. The upper rooms are beautifully furnished as Victorian bedroom and nursery, and the basement presents a Victorian scullery, pantry, kitchen and laundry. Do visit even if you have never heard of the 'Planets Suite'! *Open all year, Tue to Fri 12noon–5.30p.m. Sat 11a.m.–5.30p.m. Admission free.*

Pittville Pump Room Museum: The approach is by the fine gardens and lake of The Long Walk, established by the enterprising and sad Joseph Pitt, and provides the perfect approach to the magnificent pump room, now beautifully restored and in the care of Cheltenham Art Gallery and Museums. The upper rooms contain a collection which seeks to illustrate Cheltenham's history from the 1780s to the present day by changes in fashion. Costumes, graphics and photographs. *Open April to Oct. Tues to Sun, 10.30a.m.–5.30p.m. Admission charge.* On the ground floor is the marble pump with the long handles used to draw up the waters from the well eighty feet below. Today you just turn a tap – plastic mugs provided. Good health!

Symbols

▬▬▬▬▬	Footpath-Touring route
▬ ▬ ▬ ▬	Footpath-Touring alternative route
·–·–➤	other paths
≺	signposts
(SP)	signpost details
┼┼┼┼┼	fence
ᐱᐯᐱᐯ	wall
αΩΩαΩΩ	hedge
αΩΩ▭αΩΩ	gate
αΩΩ▮ αΩΩ	stile
⊣ ⊢	bridge
~~	stream
⏚	boggy
▲	steeply up
△	steeply down
─×──×─	overhead lines
♤♤♤	trees, deciduous
ᐱᐱᐱ	trees, coniferous
△	trig point
☩	church
▦	building
▪	building mentioned in text
(8)	Miles from overnight stop
[16 km]	Kilometres from overnight stop

🛏	accommodation, economy
🛏	accommodation, medium
🛏	accommodation, not cheap
🍺	pub
🍺	recommended pub
🍷	licensed
☕	refreshments
🍴	snack meals
✕	restaurant
□	open all year
M/O	open March to October, etc.
▭	specially recommended
⭘	recommended start time showing time to allow for walk
☎	telephone
🚕	taxi
🚌	bus
𝒊	information
🏰	castle
(P)	car-parking
🚻	toilets
😊	Guardian Angel
⛺	camping
YH	youth hostel

Thanks

A great deal of willing help and advice has been given by many people to make this Footpath-Touring with Ken Ward guide possible, for which I am most grateful.

Special thanks to Don Hildred, Ramblers Association, Stratford-upon-Avon; David Clark, Cheltenham Rambling Club; John Wigner, Rights of Way Inspector, and L.W.A. Rendall, Warwickshire County Council; Nigel Hayes, of the Footpath Section, Cotswold Wardens of Gloucestershire County Council; V.E. Jones, County Engineer and Planning Officer; and C.D. Beck, Hereford and Worcester County Council.